ILLUSTRATED HIS … ER

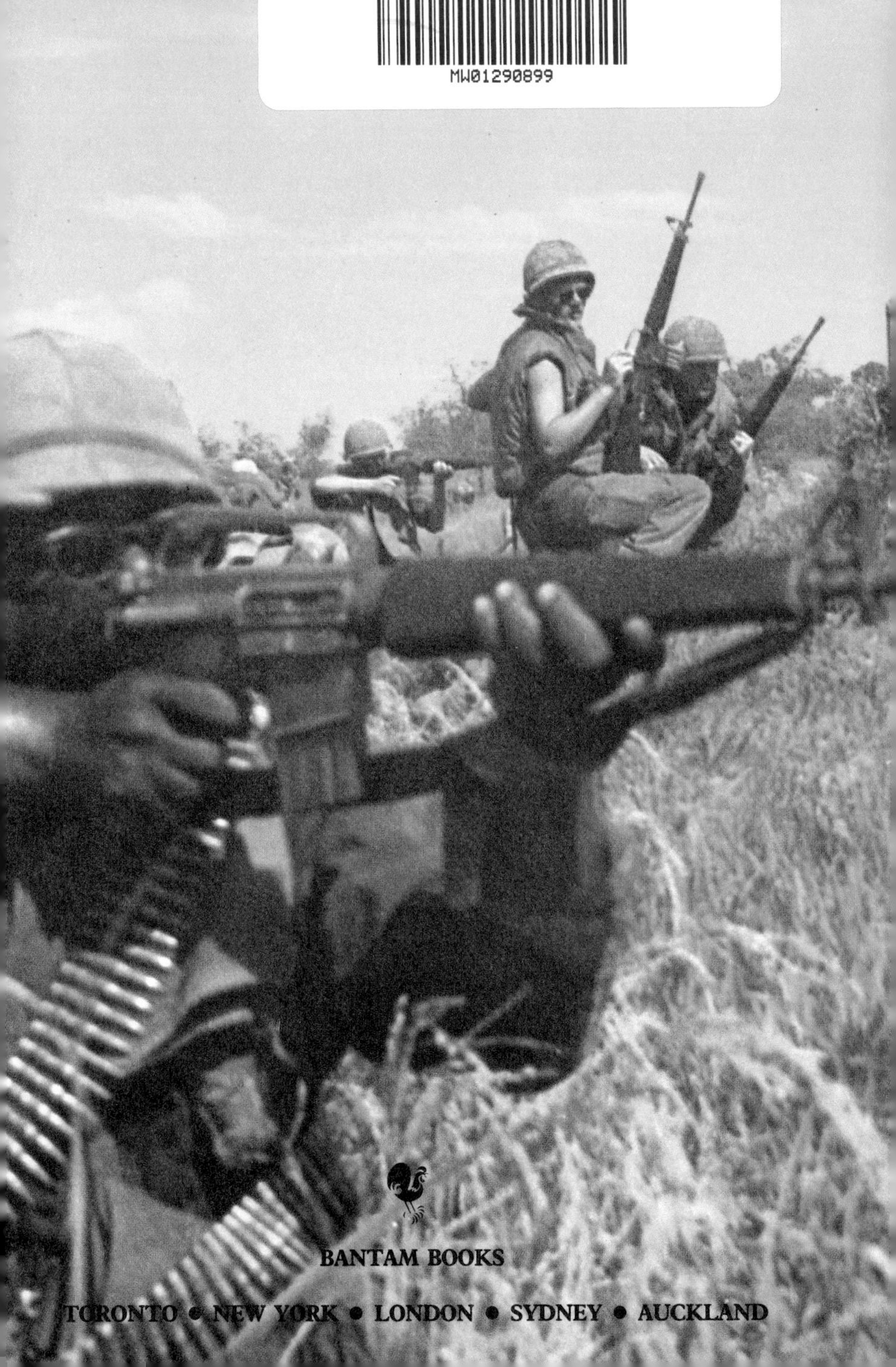

BANTAM BOOKS

TORONTO • NEW YORK • LONDON • SYDNEY • AUCKLAND

PERSONAL FIREPOWER

by
Edward C. Ezell

BLOOP TUBE ATTACHED

A soldier with the 2nd Battalion, 502d Infantry, 101st Airborne Brigade recons by fire with his M-16A1 rifle-mounted 40mm XM-148 grenade launcher during operations in Quang Ngai province. US troops discovered that the enemy was more likely to break cover when reconned by fire by a hail of 40mm high-explosive grenades rather than M-16 rifle fire. The simple to operate XM-148 was withdrawn in late 1967 because of safety defects. But the XM-148 had proved the need for a rifle-mounted grenade launcher and two years later the XM-203 was introduced.

THE M-60

A two-man Marine machine gun team of the 3d Battalion, 5th Marines, fires on an NVA position in a nearby treeline in March 1968. The M-60 machine gun entered Vietnam service in March 1965 with the arrival of the US Marines. The weapon, which fired the standard 7.62 × 51mm NATO cartridge, was not issued to ARVN infantry battalions until the end of 1969.

SHOOTER

A sniper with the 3d Battalion, 7th Marines, rests his bolt-action Model 700 Remington on his helmet while his spotter scans for a Viet Cong target. Snipers could and, routinely, did hit targets up to 900 meters distant. The Marine Corps premier Vietnam-era sniper was Sergeant Carlos Hathcock with 93 confirmed kills.

NIGHT SIGHT

An infantryman takes aim with a rifle fitted with a Starlight scope. Vietnam was the proving ground for light-intensifying devices which enabled soldiers to see the enemy in the dark. The introduction of the lightweight Starlight scope which detected and then converted any available contrast in light into signals capable of amplification up to 60,000 times revolutionized night operations, providing US troops with devices able to "see" over ranges from 300-1200 meters.

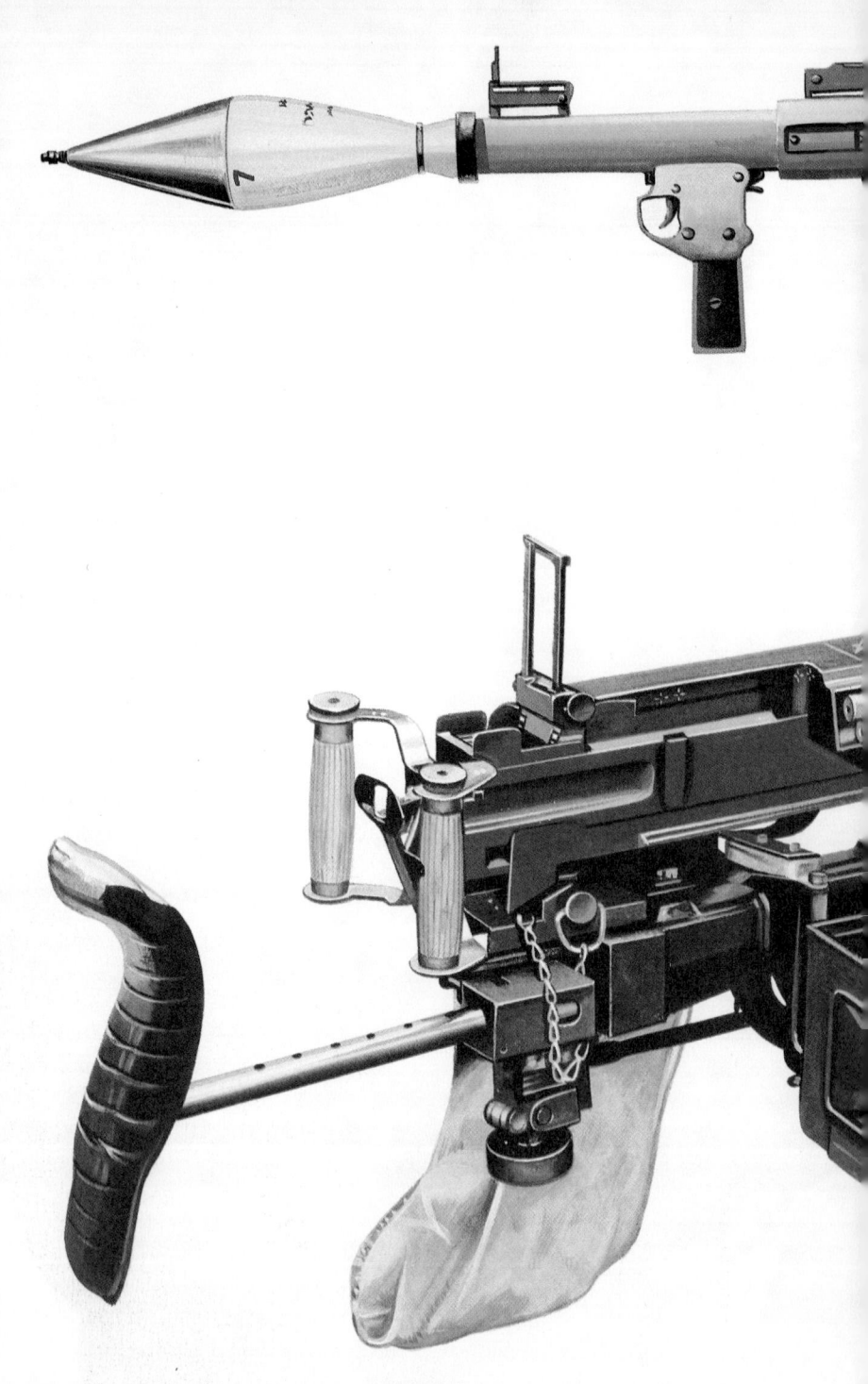

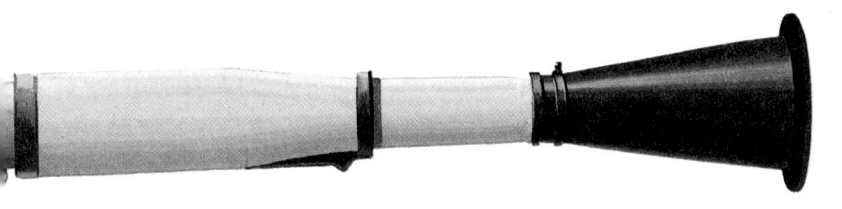

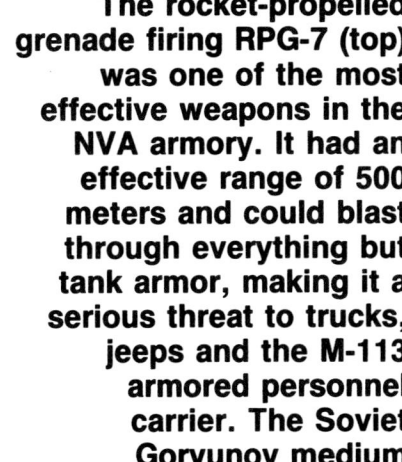

ENEMY ARMS

The rocket-propelled grenade firing RPG-7 (top) was one of the most effective weapons in the NVA armory. It had an effective range of 500 meters and could blast through everything but tank armor, making it a serious threat to trucks, jeeps and the M-113 armored personnel carrier. The Soviet Goryunov medium machine gun (below) was introduced by NVA forces post-1960. Here it is shown without its tank mounting.

EDITOR-IN-CHIEF: Ian Ballantine

SERIES EDITOR: Richard Grant.
SERIES ASSOCIATE: Richard Ballantine.
PHOTO RESEARCH: John Moore.
DIAGRAMS: John Batchelor and Peter Williams. MAPS: Kim Williams.
PRODUCED BY: The Up & Coming Publishing Company, Bearsville, New York.

PERSONAL FIREPOWER
THE ILLUSTRATED HISTORY OF THE VIETNAM WAR
A Bantam Book/ September 1988

ACKNOWLEDGEMENTS
*This book is the result of years of working in the field of military small arms
history. Numerous individuals within the US military and American industry
have assisted the research. To them all a collective thank you is given.
I especially wish to thank the staffs of the US Army Military History
Institute, Carlisle Barracks, Pennsylvania, and the Armed Forces History
Division, National Museum of American History, Smithsonian Institution,
Washington, DC. Any errors, inadvertent or otherwise, are solely my
responsibility.*

Edward C. Ezell
Washington, DC

*Photographs for this book were selected from the Department of Defense
Public Affairs Office, and the archives of DAVA, Military Archives Research
Service, and the Small Arms of the World.*

Library of Congress Cataloging-in-Publication Data

Ezell, Edward Clinton.
Personal firepower.

(The illustrated history of the Vietnam War)
1. Vietnamese conflict, 1961-1975.   2. Firearms
—Vietnam.   I. Title.   II. Series.
DS557.7.E96 1988   959.704'3   88-19322
ISBN 0-553-34549-4

Published simultaneously in the United States and Canada

*Bantam Books are published by Bantam Books, a division of Bantam Doubleday Dell
Publishing Group, Inc. Its trademark, consisting of the words "Bantam Books" and
the portrayal of a rooster, is Registered in U.S. Patent and Trademark Office and in
other countries. Marca Registrada. Bantam Books, 666 Fifth Avenue, New York, New
York 10103.*

PRINTED IN THE UNITED STATES OF AMERICA

CW0 9 8 7 6 5 4 3 2 1

Contents

From the barrel of a gun

WARS ARE NOT SIMPLY WON by the amount of materiel delivered to and expended in the war zone. If that had been the case, the United States ought to have been able to obtain its goals in Southeast Asia. But weapons and the firepower they produce are an essential element of the equation for success in combat. For 25 years, the American taxpayer supported a massive flow of weapons and munitions into that region. Less widely publicized but just as large were the equally huge movements of Soviet and Chinese war materiel into the hands of the North Vietnamese and Viet Cong fighters.

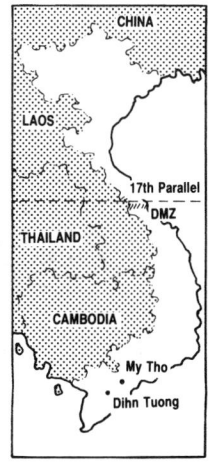

Hidden beneath the jungle's triple canopy along the "Ho Chi Minh Trail," and secreted aboard coastal shipping and river sampans, hundreds of thousands of tons of weapons, ammunition, and foodstuffs were moved southward into the war zone below the 17th Parallel. Not all of the troops fighting the South Vietnamese forces were full time beneficiaries of the North Vietnamese supply system. There were major disadvantages in being located at the end of the logistic trail.

During the mid-1960s, Viet Cong troops in the Mekong Delta, at the end of a very long and tenuous supply line, generally struggled to keep themselves supplied. Typically, the 693 soldiers of the VC 514th Main Force Battalion, operating in the Mekong's Dinh Tuong Province, relied on Hanoi, local resources, and their own wits for their war materiel, equipment, and food. American intelligence estimated that 95 percent of VC ordnance came from the North, with about five percent being manufactured in the South.

The 55 percent of the men of 514th Battalion who had weapons, possessed a mixed bag of small arms. In addition to pistols (9) and submachine guns (30) issued to officers and non-commissioned officers, the men of the 514th's three companies carried the following small arms in 1966: the locally designated "red stock" rifle, better known as the K-44 or the 7.62mm Soviet Model 44 Mosin Nagant bolt-action carbine (162); the US .30 caliber M-1 carbine (87); the US .30 caliber M-1 rifle (Garand) (27); the French 7.5mm MAS 1936 bolt-action rifle (27); an unspecified 7.62mm automatic rifle (27); and an unspecified 12.7mm machine gun (6). As support weapons, the 514th had six Chinese Type 36 57mm recoilless rifles, and six Chinese Type 31 60mm mortars. In addition, they possessed substantial numbers of hand and rifle grenades.

Even under the best of circumstances, Viet Cong troops operating in the Mekong Delta could expect ammunition resupply to take from 30 to 60 days from the time it was requested. To reduce the quantities of ammunition that had to be moved south to the Delta, by January 1966, the 514th Main Force Battalion had ordnance and munitions

support provided by a local Viet Cong company, the 518th. Operating the My Tho Province work site, its 120 personnel ran a professional organization specializing in grenade, petard, and mine production for the 514th Battalion.

Explosives and other critical materiels came from dud bombs and other munitions that were scavenged from the field after South Vietnamese operations. From these slim pickings, the Viet Cong forces in the Mekong Delta were able to supplement their meager supply of ammunition. Weapon repairs were carried out in similar field workshops.

Despite limited supplies of ammunition for all types of weapons, VC soldiers rarely ran out of cartridges while fighting. Engagements with South Vietnamese forces were carefully chosen. And the duration of most engagements was predetermined by the amount of available ammunition. When attacking, the VC fighter generally reserved enough ammunition to cover his withdrawal. In the event

NIGHT ASSAULT: **The Viet Cong moved and fought mainly at night, deriving their firepower from such basic weapons as the 7.62 × 39mm RPD light machine gun, (left) and the AK-47, being fired by the soldier on the right during this bridge assault near Cu Chi.**

19

Grease gun —A captured black pajama-clad Viet Cong guerrilla holds an M-3A1 "grease gun" above his head. The US .45 cal. submachine gun, was favored by local defense forces and American advisers on patrol because it was compact and easy to carry. Its major shortcoming was its lack of killing power at ranges greater than 100 meters.

of being surprised by a larger South Vietnamese unit, the Viet Cong would often bury their weapons when they ran out of cartridges. Following a hasty withdrawal, they would recover those arms when the government troops had moved on.

The men of the 514th Main Force Battalion had a reputation for being ferocious fighters. This was the force that had defeated the relatively new Army of the Republic of Vietnam (ARVN) on 2 January 1963 in its first major battle. Ap Bac, on the Plain of Reeds, about 60 kilometers southeast of Saigon in the Delta, became synonymous with ARVN failings and Viet Cong capabilities on the battlefield. The ARVN commanders had poor intelligence information regarding the location and number of the VC. This shortcoming canceled out the advantages of superior armor, helicopter, and air cover available to the 2,500 South Vietnamese troops that went up against the 514th Battalion. The battle ran against the ARVN forces from the first shot.

The commander of the 514th knew his terrain, he planned his defense well, and his troops fought skillfully. As an example, his well-trained gunners used their two 12.7mm (.50 caliber) machine guns to shoot down five helicopters and to damage all but one of the others involved in the fight.

When the battle was over and the Viet Cong drifted away from the field at nightfall, they had suffered some 50 killed in action (KIA), 36 captured, and an unknown number of wounded. On the allied side, there were 66 KIA (including three Americans) and 115 wounded (including six Americans). Although the numbers suggest a draw, the fact that the VC had taken on forces five times their size indicated that communist forces were capable of putting up a good fight as long as they had the proper equipment and sufficient ammunition.

The point was made clearly in American news dispatches.

Looking only at the conflict in the Delta, one could mistake the war in Vietnam as having been a lopsided contest between a small semi-industrial state (North Vietnam) and a nation that was an industrial superpower (United States). In reality there were several types of conflicts occurring at any one time in Indochina. Taken together these

514TH VIETCONG PROVINCE MAIN FORCE BATTALION: WEAPONS (CIRCA 1966)

Number of Weapons

Weapon	Basic Load (Rounds)	Recon squad + Battalion HQ	3 Companies	Total
7.62 × 25mm pistol	NA	3	6	9
7.62 × 25mm submachine gun	200	3	27	30
7.62 × 33mm (.30 caliber) M-1 carbine	300a	9	78	87
7.62 × 54mmR K-44 or "Red stock" rifle	100a	-	162	162
7.62 × 63mm (.30 caliber) M-1 (Garand) rifle	250	-	27	27
7.5 × 54mm MAS 36 bolt-action rifle.	100a	-	27	27
7.62 × ??mm automatic rifle (model unknown)	800	-	27	27
12.7 × 108mm heavy machine gun	500	-	6	6
Type 36 PRC 57mm recoilless rifle (Copy of US M-18)	4	-	6	6
Type 31 PRC 60mm mortar (Copy of US 60mm mortar)	4	-	6	6
Hand grenades	500 per company			1500
Rifle grenades				2208

a = Eight rifle grenades were issued with each of these 276 rifles for a total of 2,208 rifle grenades.

Vietnam conflicts made up a war that pitted the war materiel producing capacities of the United States against the military industries of the Soviet Union, China, and North Vietnam.

The length of the conflict afforded the various belligerents opportunities to experiment with both weapons and tactics. While the Americans and South Vietnamese tried more new pieces of hardware than their adversaries from the North, there were concerted efforts on both sides to find new ways of killing off the enemy. This book covers the span of years from the first shots fired by French Foreign Legionnaires on 22 September 1945 to the final shots discharged by the troops of the Army of the Republic of Vietnam at the end of April 1975.

First shots

The French years, 1945-54

THE SEEDS of the conflict that would eventually embroil US forces in an 11-year war in Indochina began in September 1940 when Imperial Japanese Army troops crossed the border from China into the French colony of Indochina, which embraced Vietnam. The move enabled Japan to consolidate its hold on Southeast Asia.

Under an agreement between Japan and Nazi-occupied Vichy France, the Vichy troops were allowed to maintain control of Indochina for the next five years on behalf of the Japanese. To the indigenous people of Vietnam, who had already shown the first flickerings of a desire for independence, this political-military arrangement was far from acceptable; the French would still remain their immediate colonial masters, albeit as servants of the Japanese. The more politically active Vietnamese—many of them, ironically, from the first generation of Vietnamese to be educated by the French, who wanted them to fill the ranks of junior civil servants—organized a resistance movement that was to play a significant post-war role.

The weapons available to Vietnamese resistance fighters at the beginning of the French-Vietnamese war represented the wide variety of infantry arms used throughout Asia in the first four decades of this century. But as the conflict between the occupying powers and the independence movement escalated, first one side and then the other would improve its infantry equipment. This process began slowly in the 1945-50 period; sped up in the years 1950-55; accelerated even more sharply between 1964 and 1969; and stabilized thereafter.

At each increase in the number of combat troops, the burdens on each side's logistic systems grew. A

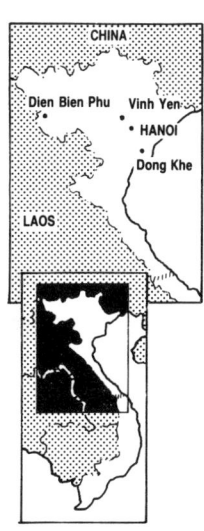

First shots

COLONIAL POWER: Pith-helmeted French troops march through a Vietnam hamlet in the early thirties, in a typical everyday display of colonial power. Their rifles are the 8 × 50.5mm Model 1902 Mannlicher Berthier rifles of the so-called ''Indochina Model.'' Later, weapons like these, which were first brought to Indochina for the purpose of maintaining the colonial status quo, would be used to drive the French out of Vietnam.

considerable amount of American military activity during the years 1964-72 was devoted to staunching the flow of weapons and related materiel to the Viet Cong and North Vietnamese Army forces operating in South Vietnam. One of the many reasons that the war was won by the North can be traced to their ability to continue to deliver the tools of war to their fighters in the field, especially in the face of steady American bombing and ground operations against their supply lines.

When British troops arrived in Saigon on 12 September 1945 to accept the surrender of the

Japanese in Indochina, they discovered that Ho Chi
Minh, then emerging as leader of the Vietnamese
independence movement, and his "People's
Congress" had declared the existence of the
Independent Democratic Republic of Vietnam ten
days earlier. Much of the area near the Chinese
border and around the key cities of Hanoi and
Haiphong was under the control of Ho's Vietminh
(Viet Nam Doc Lap Dong Minh Hoi, or League for
the Independence of Viet Nam). Within weeks,
French colonials and various Vietnamese nationalist
groups began contesting Ho Chi Minh's Vietminh

(already 31,000 strong) for control of the Vietnamese portion of Indochina.

In the South, in addition to using his own Indian and Gurkha troops, British General Douglas Gracey decided to employ both Imperial Japanese Army units and 1,400 French troops (formerly prisoners of war) to maintain order. At first, the French forces, mostly Foreign Legionnaires, were armed with British small arms. Units from these latter troops attacked Saigon city hall on 22 September and expelled the Vietminh's Executive Committee residing there. On 24 September, General Jacques Phillipe Leclerc, newly appointed French commander in Vietnam, declared: "We have come to claim our inheritance." Thus began the war that was to last nearly ten years for the French and still another 20 years for the Americans.

An uneasy truce between French and Vietminh forces came to an end in December 1946, when a Vietminh revolt signaled the start of low-level guerrilla warfare. General Vo Nguyen Giap, the Vietminh military commander, was aware that the French possessed materiel and manpower resource superiority over his fledgling fighting force. Still he was confident that his forces could make up for materiel and manpower shortages by gaining the tactical edge.

Gen. Vo Nguyen Giap —Architect of the Vietminh victory over the French at Dien Bien Phu and later to become the Defense Minister of North Vietnam.

Giap was not impressed by the tactical skills of the French commanders under Leclerc. Giap believed that his forces (regulars and irregulars numbering about 60,000 at the end of 1946) could ultimately defeat the French provided they could keep the pot boiling through selective small actions against exposed French units. Such a protracted struggle would allow the Vietminh to build support among the people of Indochina, as they incessantly picked away at the French. During 1947-48, the Vietminh managed to prevent being completely expelled from the territories they claimed. In addition, they inflicted a number of humiliating defeats on French forces in the field.

Despite the French efforts in 1948 to create an autonomous Vietnam within the French Union under the leadership of Emperor Bao Dai, the Vietminh movement grew in power and popularity. The French responded by introducing more of their own troops. By the end of 1949 the French had some

150,000 troops in Vietnam, up from 94,000 in 1947. French forces were armed with American and German hardware salvaged from the war in Europe. Giap's forces, which now numbered about 60,000 regulars and about 100,000 militia, were equipped with an equally eccentric assortment of surplus weapons.

Vietminh forces relied mainly upon weapons acquired from the defeated Japanese Army. Some weapons were of French origin, the Vietminh having received supplies via French intelligence operatives during World War II. They also managed to steal arms and ammunition from the Vietnamese militia units of Emperor Bao Dai. An even smaller number, despite French accusations to the contrary, had come from the American Office of Strategic Services (OSS). By March 1946, the Vietminh possessed an estimated 36,000 small arms. Their weapons doubled by the end of the year. Although their small arms arsenal continued to grow, the Vietminh fought a continuous battle of supply versus loss in these early years.

But the Vietminh had next to nothing in the way of heavy weaponry. Artillery and armor were

BREN GUNNER:
The French used a variety of weapons in the early period of the war against the Vietminh. Here a French outpost team watches for enemy movement. They are armed with a British .303 cal. Bren gun, a light support weapon that proved popular with both the French and the Vietminh, who captured many of these weapons.

JUNK FORCE: A flotilla of dugout canoes carry Vietminh guerrillas across a river in the Delta during the years of the fight against the French. The scene, a low-key display of force, probably put on for propaganda purposes, illustrates the potpourri of small arms employed by the Vietminh. The soldier standing, wearing a trilby hat, is holding a US .30 cal. M-1 carbine. The others are armed with British .303 cal. SMLE rifles.

virtually unknown in the Vietminh tables of organization and equipment. While the French could deploy infantry units supported by some antique artillery, and a small number of armored vehicles, Vietminh cadres were limited to the firepower provided by their small arms—mainly bolt-action rifles and a jumble of aging machine guns. The Vietminh had only a few old mortars for artillery support. Artillery was a priority item on the Vietminh shopping list.

This hardware imbalance forced Giap's commanders to rely upon attacks of short duration

on those occasions when they could muster a numerical advantage over the French. Vietminh forces moved through the jungle in loose formations, only coming together in a concentrated attacking force when the carefully selected objective had been reached. They launched sudden and brief attacks; doing as much damage as quickly as possible. Then they disengaged, withdrew, dispersed, and disappeared from the battlefield.

The French found this type of hit-and-run warfare frustrating and expensive in terms of manpower and equipment. Instead of being able to concentrate their

First delivery —A French soldier, armed with a US .30 cal. M-1 carbine, works his way through heavy Vietnamese undergrowth. The light and compact M-1 was included in the first batch of weapons supplied by the US to the French under a new agreement implemented in August 1950.

forces at any one point, they were forced to scatter their troops to maintain security. Combatting the Vietminh was a constant drain on manpower with French troops used for patrolling roads, guarding supply lines, and conducting limited searches for guerrilla strongholds.

Vietminh arms supplies were boosted with the Christmas 1949 defeat of the Nationalist Chinese Army (Kuomintang) by the Chinese Communist People's Liberation Army on the mainland of China. Now that they had won their own war, the Chinese communists were able to supply Giap's Vietminh with additional equipment for his troops. As before, much of this materiel was ex-Japanese World War II stock. However, some of the aid from the Chinese also included such essential items as American M-18 57mm recoilless rifles, 60mm mortars, light artillery, antiaircraft weapons, and a variety of mines and hand grenades. French military intelligence officers only slowly appreciated the threat posed by these Vietminh arms and munitions.

When they realized what was happening, the French severely underestimated both the numbers of weapons provided and the speed with which the Vietminh were able to put them into the field. The French believed they could offset the Vietminh buildup by obtaining more and better weapons for their troops from the United States.

President Harry S. Truman approved the first American military aid package, $15 million, on 10 March 1950. Four months later, on 27 July 1950, a month after hostilities had started in Korea, President Truman ordered Department of Defense acceleration of military assistance to Indochina. By 1952, America was supporting between 50 and 60 percent of the financial burden of the Indochina War through military assistance to the French. During the years 1950-54, the United States provided about $3 billion to finance the French military in Indochina.

On 3 August 1950, a US Military Assistance Advisory Group (MAAG) of 35 men arrived in Vietnam to begin instructing French and Vietnamese troops in the use of American military hardware. Despite early friction between the Americans and the French, the flow of American equipment began to have an impact on the war.

Initial deliveries included .30 caliber (7.62 × 33mm) M-1 carbines, .30 caliber (7.62 × 63mm) M-1 rifles, .30 caliber (7.62 × 63mm) M-1918A2 Browning automatic rifles, .30 caliber (7.62 × 63mm) M-1919A4 machine guns, and other World War II US infantry equipment. These deliveries began an uninterrupted 25-year flow of US military materiel to Southeast Asia.

Meanwhile, General Giap had received sufficient arms and instructional assistance from the Soviet Union and the People's Republic of China to organize three full-sized and properly equipped infantry divisions—about 35,000 fighting men. At the same time Giap's staff created a logistic infrastructure to support his troops with food, ammunition, and other supplies. Giap could now shift from guerrilla raids to full-scale conventional battles. This was an extremely dangerous development for the French, but once again their intelligence did not assess it properly.

In September 1950, Giap began experimenting with a new type of campaign when he concentrated an infantry brigade against Dong Khe, a small French outpost near the Chinese border. Garrisoned by about 250 French Foreign Legionnaires, Dong Khe was first softened up by concentrated mortar fire. When this barrage lifted, the Vietminh infantry

PIPETALK:

A Vietnamese member of the French colonial forces on an intelligence-gathering mission waits while an elderly Vietnamese smokes a native *bong*. The young soldier is armed with a French 7.5 × 54mm MAS Mle. 1936 bolt-action rifle. It was one of many small arms produced by Manufacture d'Armes de Saint-Etienne, a key supplier of pistols, rifles, and submachine guns to the French forces.

LINES OF SUPPLY: Two Vietminh guerrillas, armed with US .30 cal. M-1917 Enfield rifles, take cover behind a dyke on the edge of a rice paddy. In all probability the rifles were supplied to the Vietminh by the Chinese Communists who had captured them from Chinese Nationalist forces during the civil war.

attacked in successive waves, then withdrew to permit another bombardment. Then the Vietminh infantry attacked once again. A few French survivors escaped, leaving Dong Khe in the hands of Giap's troops.

This French defeat was rapidly followed by other bold and successful Vietminh attacks on a border post and on a French relief force moving up to retake the fallen posts. The 4,000-man relief force was completely destroyed. Within a few weeks Giap had driven the French forces away from the Chinese-North Vietnamese border. The Vietminh now had control over supply routes to China. In the process, Vietminh troops had inflicted huge casualties

(nearly 6,000 killed, wounded, or captured), and captured vast amounts of equipment, acquiring between 8,000 and 10,000 rifles, 1,000 machine guns, 125 mortars, 13 artillery pieces, over 400 trucks, and sizable amounts of ammunition.

Being routed in the northern provinces finally alerted the French that they could lose Vietnam if the military situation did not change radically. In an effort to alter the course of the conflict, the French government in Paris sent General Jean de Lattre de Tassigny, a well-respected and competent soldier, to take command. The autumn debacles also alerted American leaders, who were having troubles of their own stemming the tide of North Korean

THE ARMS RACE

FRENCH SMALL ARMS

11.43 × 23mm US M-1A1 submachine gun
11.43 × 23mm US M-3/Chinese Type 36 submachine gun
8 × 50.5mmR Model 1902 Lebel (Indochina Model) rifle
7.92 × 57mm German Mauser 98K rifle
7.5 × 54 MAS Mle. 1936 bolt action rifle
7.5 × 54mm MAS Mle. 1949 self-loading
7.62 × 33mm US M-1 carbine
7.62 × 63mm US M-1 rifle
7.5 × 54mm MAC Mle. 1924/29 LMG
7.5 × 54mm MAC Mle. 1931A LMG
7.7 × 53mm UK Bren gun
7.92 × 57mm German MG 34 LMG
7.62 × 63mm US M-1918A2 BAR
7.62 × 63mm US M-1919A4 LMG
12.7 × 99mm US M-2 Heavy Barrel MG

aggression. With 150,000 men in Korea, Americans such as General Douglas MacArthur could not understand why the French were unable to get the upper hand in Indochina. During 1951, the increased flow of American fighting equipment relieved the burden on the struggling French logistic system.

One of General de Lattre's first moves was to set about creating an effective Vietnamese National Army. Although there had been some Vietnamese units created in 1948-49, the main fighting burden was borne by French forces. In May 1950, there were only about 16,000 Vietnamese regulars. General de Lattre planned for a 34-battalion, 60,000-man fighting force. Progress was slow. By May 1951 there were less than 40,000 Vietnamese in 24 partially staffed battalions. Only seven had Vietnamese officers. Meanwhile, General Giap was about to start a new offensive.

General de Lattre's arrival and the good use he made of his new American equipment forced Giap to refocus his plans. Frequent French air patrols caused the Vietminh commanders to be reluctant to move their troops by day; such movement attracted immediate shelling by artillery and bombardment from the air with iron and napalm bombs.

Attempting to bring the situation to a head, General Giap decided to gamble with a set-piece attack on a French outpost. In January 1951, Giap brought up two of his three divisions (about 22,000 men) against the garrison at Vinh Yen, some 50 kilometers northeast of Hanoi. De Lattre, receiving early warning of Giap's concentration, mustered 8,000 troops, and moved to meet Giap's forces. In the ensuing battle Giap lost a major part of his force (6,000 killed and 8,000 wounded) before his commanders were able to break off the engagement and retreat.

A large part of this French success was due to the timely arrival of American weapons and equipment. In just one week in early January 1951, the United States had delivered twenty M-24 tanks, forty 105mm howitzers, and sizable quantities of conventional and napalm bombs, howitzer ammunition, and a variety of small caliber weapons. Without this hardware, the French would have been unable to defend their bases.

Later, in March, Giap tried again to mount an attack in the Haiphong region. Once again he miscalculated the relative effectiveness of his own troops and that of his enemy. French forces beat off all of these attacks, and their spirits soared. However, the French commanders failed to follow up their victories by pursuing and destroying Giap's remaining troops. The prevailing French operational

First shots

STANDARD ARMS: French troops wade across a river during the war against the Vietminh. As part of a drive towards standardization all the troops are carrying French weapons. The soldier in the immediate foreground has his 7.5 × 54mm MAS 36 bolt-action rifle over his shoulder. In front of him, to his left, a colleague carries a 7.5 × 54mm MAC Mle. 1924/29 light machine gun. This very popular squad automatic weapon saw service for many years in Indochina, used by forces of all political persuasions.

concept remained static defense. Persistent tactical reliance upon mechanized infantry tied French troops to the few improved roads. Their insistent use of defensive lines encircling Hanoi and Haiphong gave the initiative back to the Vietminh.

Giap made two further large-scale attacks against the Hanoi area. Both were repulsed by the French, largely through the skillful use of American-provided artillery pieces. After these French victories there was a period of quiet. Both sides were exhausted. Vietminh leaders squabbled internally about the causes of their defeats. They spent the

summer of 1951 reorganizing and re-equipping. The French, whose morale was much improved by their victories, used the time to strengthen their forces.

In September 1951, General de Lattre visited Washington, D.C., to request more military assistance. Previously promised equipment had not been delivered because the Americans were having problems regearing production of war materiel. De Lattre managed to get American agreement to expedite the delivery of ammunition, vehicles, and specific types of small arms such as .45 caliber (11.43 × 23mm) Thompson submachine guns. Between de

Lattre's September 1951 visit and February 1952, the French received over 130,000 tons of equipment, including 53 million rounds of ammunition, 8,000 general purpose vehicles, 200 aircraft, 3,500 radio sets, and 14,000 automatic weapons. A year later those totals had risen to 900 combat vehicles, 15,000 general purpose vehicles, 2,500 artillery pieces, 9,000 radio sets, 24,000 automatic weapons, and 75,000 other small arms.

Such huge demands for materiel caused the US Military Assistance Advisory Group to look into the possibility of manufacturing some hardware in Vietnam. Some groups, such as the Cao Dai religious sect, were already making small arms, mortars, mines, and hand grenades in the South. This proposal, much promoted by the Americans, was never seriously entertained by the French. By mid-1952, the Americans abandoned this idea. Instead, they continued to ship arms and ammunition halfway around the world.

To the detriment of the French cause, General de Lattre died of cancer in January 1952. His death came just as his troops were carrying the battle to the Vietminh. As French forces left their Hanoi havens and occupied fortified outposts, Giap once again concentrated his forces and attacked. At this point the French, under the command of General Raoul Salan, began to bring troops from the southern half of Vietnam into the war. The Americans supported this concept and assisted in the training of Vietnamese personnel.

The deciding confrontation between the Vietminh and the French came in the spring of 1954. The origins of the battle of Dien Bien Phu went back to 1953, when the Vietminh had launched a short-lived campaign into neighboring Laos. This action had upset both the French and the Laotians. The French commander, General Henri Navarre, set out to block the Vietminh's reinforcement and supply route, which led into Laos. To accomplish this, late in 1953, he sent three parachute battalions (about 3,000 men) to occupy Dien Bien Phu, a small village some 320 kilometers inside Vietminh-controlled country.

The outpost at Dien Bien Phu consisted of two airstrips with three fortified strong points. These latter positions were protected in turn by four smaller outposts. Once the position was constructed,

French legacy —A member of the American Division holds a VC-modified French-manufactured 7.62 × 25mm MAT 49 submachine gun just turned in by a young Vietnamese boy. The year is 1970 and the weapon had been in-country for at least 16 years.

LOCAL V.C.   VŪNG V.C.

THE OPPOSITION:
A mixture of old weapons continued to be used by the Viet Cong long after the French left Vietnam. This board, assembled in 1965, includes the 9 × 19mm MAT 49 (top left), a US .45 cal. M-1A1 Thompson, without stock (lower left), and a modified Chinese 7.62 × 25mm Type 50 submachine gun, a K-50 M. The rifles from the top are: 7.92 × 57mm Mauser98K, US .30 cal. M-1903, 12-gauge single barrel shotgun, US .30 M-1 carbine, and US .30 M-1918A2 Browning automatic rifle.

more troops (totaling about 15,000), complete with artillery, light tanks, and ground support aircraft, were flown in. The surrounding terrain was so hilly and the roads so poor that it was the only way equipment could be brought in. Or so it seemed. The French hoped that this garrison would incite an attack by the Vietminh. When they set upon the French troops, the Vietminh were to be destroyed by superior firepower.

On 13 March 1954, the Vietminh forces began their assault on the French positions. The Vietminh preceded their onslaught with an intense artillery barrage. Its ferocity totally astonished the French. Where had the guns come from? They could not believe that any military force could possibly have manhandled such large caliber artillery pieces through the surrounding terrain. But the Vietminh had done just that. There ensued a protracted siege, which culminated on 7 May with a French surrender. The immediate cost of the battle at Dien Bien Phu was some 7,184 men killed, wounded, or missing, and 11,000 men led off to captivity. The Vietminh suffered 20,000 casualties, including 8,000 dead. With a total of 35,000 men dead and 48,000 wounded on their side since 1945, the French decided to withdraw from Indochina. In accordance with a pact hammered out in Geneva, the last French soldier left the region in 1956.

The legacy of 1945

CHAPTER

3

Small arms 1945-54

THE WEAPONS used in the first ten years of the Southeast Asian conflict were a varied assortment from World War II. French Foreign Legion troops, traditionally responsible for the defense of Indochina, were principally armed with German and French weapons. At the outset they carried 7.92 × 57mm 98K Mauser bolt-action rifles and machine guns such as the MG-34 liberated in Europe. In time, French weapons were reintroduced. These included: the 7.5 x 54mm MAS 1936 bolt-action rifle, the 7.5 × 54mm MAS Mle. 1949 self-loading rifle, the 7.65 × 20mm MAS 1938 submachine gun, the 7.5 × 54mm Mle. 1924/29 light machine gun, and the 60mm and 81mm Brandt mortars. French parachute units employed a special version of the 7.5mm MAS 1936 rifle, in which the butt was made of aluminum and folded forward to make it more compact during a parachute drop.

In the years immediately following World War II, the 7.65mm MAS Mitrallette Modele 1938, developed at the Manufacture d'Armes de Saint-Etienne in the mid-1930s, was an early favorite of French troops on patrol. Manufactured from 1938 to 1949, most of these submachine guns had their date of manufacture stamped into the wooden stock. While the 7.65mm MAS 1938 submachine gun was a reasonably good design, its combat effectiveness was limited by its low powered 7.65mm cartridge. This particular pistol cartridge has never been used by any other major military organization. Nevertheless, the MAS 1938 was a reliable, if only moderately effective, little weapon in the early stages of the Indochina conflict, since the Vietminh were even more poorly armed. The same 7.65mm cartridge was also employed in the MAS 1935S self-

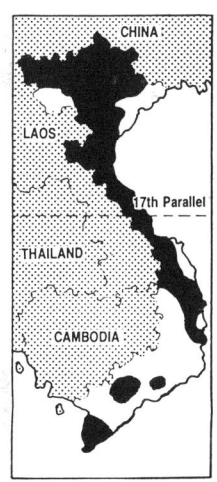

Map shows Vietminh-occupied areas (in black) before the country was partitioned along the 17th Parallel in 1954.

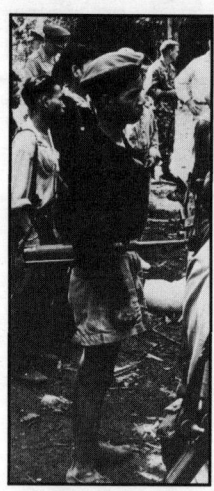

Hand-me-down —A South Vietnamese Civil Defense guard listens intently as he is instructed in the use of a grease gun. It would replace the 9 × 19mm German MP 38/40 submachine gun, slung from his shoulder. These weapons probably were brought to Vietnam in the late 1940s when the French re-equipped their forces in Indochina.

loading pistol; a modified Colt-Browning operating mechanism.

As the French-Vietnamese war intensified, other submachine guns came into play. Most common were the US .45 caliber 11.43 × 23mm Thompsons (M-1928A1 and M-1 series) and the 9 × 19mm MAT 49. The latter weapon, developed and manufactured at the French state Manufacture d'Armes de Tulle (MAT), fired the 9mm Parabellum cartridge, thus giving it more punch than the 7.65mm MAS 38 submachine gun. A very robust weapon, made from stamped sheet metal components, the MAT 49 was about .89 kg (2 pounds) heavier than the MAS 38. As with many other post-1945 submachine guns, the MAT 49 had a pistol grip squeeze safety catch that reduced the likelihood of accidental discharge when handled roughly. This submachine gun remained popular with the North Vietnamese long after the French had withdrawn from Indochina.

Upon inheriting the MAT 49 submachine guns from the French, through the Vietminh, Viet Cong armorers converted these weapons to the more readily available Soviet 7.62 × 25mm pistol/sub-machine gun cartridge. This home-grown alteration required the addition of a longer barrel (260mm vs 208mm for the standard gun), and incorporated a new 35-shot magazine. Employment of the more powerful 7.62mm cartridge raised the MAT 49's cyclic rate from 600 shots per minute to nearly 900. As late as the early 1970s, Viet Cong workshops in the Delta were fabricating spare parts for the MAT 49, in an attempt to keep them operating.

On the Vietnamese side a number of other submachine guns were pressed into service. Early on the Vietminh, and later the Viet Cong, used World War II German 9 × 19mm Maschinenpistole 38 and 40 models, more generally called MP 38s, and MP 40s, or Schmeissers by Allied forces. These German submachine guns had been brought from Europe to Indochina for the French Foreign Legion. Many fell into the hands of the Vietminh before 1954, and still more were captured after Dien Bien Phu. Later in the 1960s, these MPs were phased out of service by the North Vietnamese and Viet Cong in favor of submachine guns firing the 7.62 × 25mm cartridge or rifles using still more powerful ammunition. South Vietnamese Civil Defense forces

The legacy of 1945

BUGLE PATROL:

A Vietnamese soldier in the French colonial forces emerges from a typical Vietminh bunker and tunnel complex. He is armed with a French 7.5 × 54mm MAS Mle. 1936 bolt-action rifle and a bugle, an instrument that in the fifties still had a practical as well as a ceremonial function.

Old soldiers —These 1945-vintage weapons were captured 20 years in Bien Hoa Province 20 years after the end of World War II. In the center is a World War II German 7.92 × 57mm MG34 general purpose machine gun on an antiaircraft tripod. Also pictured are 7.62 × 54mm M-44 carbines of the type the Soviets and Chinese delivered to the Vietminh.

also employed these German submachine guns from time to time.

When the People's Republic of China began sending weapons into Vietnam in 1950, they first shipped more ex-Japanese equipment that the Chinese had removed from Japanese arsenals and depots in Manchuria in 1945. When these arms began to run short, the Chinese began sending older pattern Soviet Mosin-Nagant rifles, submachine guns, and artillery weapons. These shipments included particularly large numbers of Soviet 7.62 × 25mm PPSh41 and 7.62 × 25mm PPS43 submachine guns, ideal weapons for guerrillas. At the time these submachine guns were virtually the global trademark of communist-backed irregular forces. The combined Soviet production total of both weapons exceeded 2.5 million during World War II. As time passed, these were supplemented with their Chinese clones; Type 50 (PPSh41) and Type 43 (PPS43) submachine guns. The PPSh41 and the PPS43 may have lacked aesthetic appeal to western eyes, but both were durable and reliable. The employment of the 7.62 × 25mm cartridge, rather than the western 9 × 19mm Parabellum round, logistically tied the Vietminh to communist sources for their ammunition.

In an attempt to reduce the weight of the PPSh41/Type 50 (4.2 kg), and to make it more handy, the Viet Cong modified many of these weapons. They shortened the barrel jacket (adding a front sling swivel), attached a front sight onto the barrel, and replaced the wooden buttstock with a metal receiver cover that accepted a sliding wire stock and an AK-47-type pistol grip. The altered weapon, called the K-50 M (M for modified) weighed about .5 kg less than the PPSh41 (K-50).

The 7.5 × 54mm Manufacture Nationale d'Armes de Chatellerault Mle. 1924/29 light machine gun was a squad automatic weapon similar in type and tactical function to the American .30 caliber (7.62 × 63mm) M-1918A2 Browning automatic rifle and the British .303 caliber (7.7 × 53mm) Bren gun. As chambered for the 7.5 × 54mm cartridge it was called the Mle. 1924/29. It employed a top-mounted 30-shot box magazine, and like its American and British counterparts was actuated by a gas piston system. Although it was rather heavy (9.2 kg), it was

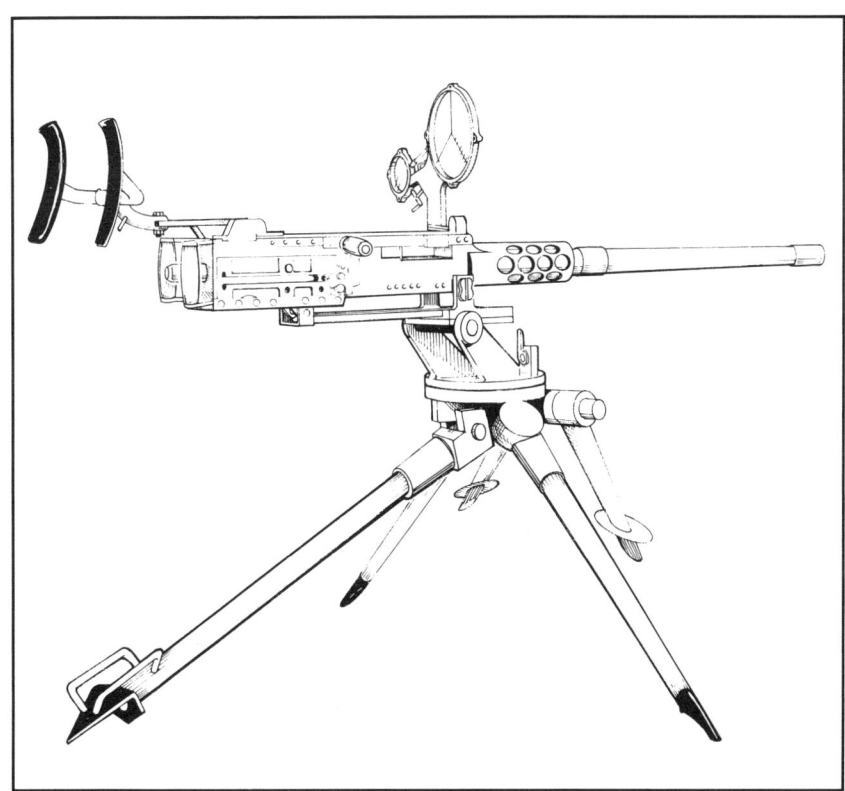

much admired by the French and later the Viet Cong for its reliability and utility as a basic fire weapon. One unique identifying feature was its two triggers; front for single shots, and rear for full automatic fire.

In the next phase of the war, from 1954 on, during which the United States played a more significant role, the quantities of American small arms shipped to Southeast Asia grew considerably.

With the exception of the blowback .45 caliber Thompson submachine gun, all the American infantry shoulder weapons were gas operated, self-loaders.

The .30 caliber (7.62 × 33mm) M-1 and M-2 carbines looked like scaled down .30 caliber (7.62 × 63mm) M-1 Garands. The carbine was a very handy weapon for both the French and their smaller stature Vietnamese troops, but its cartridge had very limited killing power even at close ranges. The 8-shot semiautomatic M-1 rifles and the 20-shot full

US-SOVIET ADAPTATION:

The Vietminh pressed many different heavy machine guns into service as antiaircraft weapons. One common adaptation was this American .50 cal (12.7 × 99mm) mounted on a Soviet DShK antiaircraft tripod complete with Soviet AA machine gun sight.

An assortment
of World War II
weapons
continued to
appear in later
years. These
arms, captured
in 1962,
included 57mm
recoilless rifles
and a French
7.5 × 54mm
Model 1931
fortress machine
gun.

automatic .30 caliber (7.62 × 63mm) M-1918A2
Browning automatic rifles (BAR) were sufficiently
powerful, but they were big and heavy (4.3 and 8.8
kg respectively).

Each of these .30 caliber weapons was created for
specific purposes. The World War II vintage
carbines, with their 15- and 30-shot magazines, were
intended to replace the pistol as the sidearm of
individual who needed a weapon, but whose primary
function was something other than combat infantryman. As time passed, both the French and the
Vietnamese used these weapons as substitutes for
the rifle and the submachine gun, roles for which
they were not well suited.

The full power .30 caliber (7.62 × 63mm) M-1 and
M-1918A2 BAR were capable of delivering substantial firepower. The effectiveness of the M-1

Garand was somewhat limited by its 8-shot en bloc clip. On the other hand, the BAR was an effective squad support weapon just as were its French and British counterparts; the 7.5mm MAC Mle. 24/29 and .303 Bren light machine guns. As a heavier support weapon, the US provided the French with .30 caliber .30-06 M-1919A4 Browning light machine guns. In time all of these weapons fell into the hands of the North Vietnamese and their southern supporters.

In the Vietminh arsenals there was an even larger variety of small caliber weapons. As noted earlier, the Vietminh began their war against the French with many weapons taken from the Japanese. At first their basic shoulder weapon was the 6.5 × 50.5mmSR Japanese Arisaka bolt-action rifle. Supporting fire was provided by a mixture of Japanese machine guns including the 6.5 × 50.5mmSR Type 11, 7.7 × 57mm Type 92, and the 7.7 × 57mm Type 99. Of these, the Type 11 had been the squad automatic weapon for Japanese forces during World War II.

As with many Japanese automatic weapons the Type 11 (1922) was based upon the operating mechanism of the French Hotchkiss machine gun. Unlike the metal strip fed French guns, the Type 11 had an unusual feed system that allowed five-round clips of 6.5mm ammunition to be dropped into a hopper that stripped the cartridges from the clips as the weapon fired. The idea behind this feeder was

HOMEMADE:
This 9 × 19mm copy of a US .45 caliber M-1911A1 was captured in the late 1950s, but was probably made by a South Vietnamese religious sect, the Cao Dai, during the French period. Homemade firearms were not uncommon during the French years in Vietnam. The South Vietnamese need for homemade arms disappeared when US military hardware started to flood into the country.

The legacy of 1945

JAPANESE SPECIALS:
The Japanese 6.5mm Type 96 (top) and the 7.7mm Type 99 (bottom) light machine guns were the favorite weapons of the Vietminh in the 1950s, and later of NVA troops. The Type 99, one of the first weapons designed specifically for the 7.7mm cartridge, was modeled after a Czech-pattern machine gun used by the Chinese Nationalist Army in the 1930s.

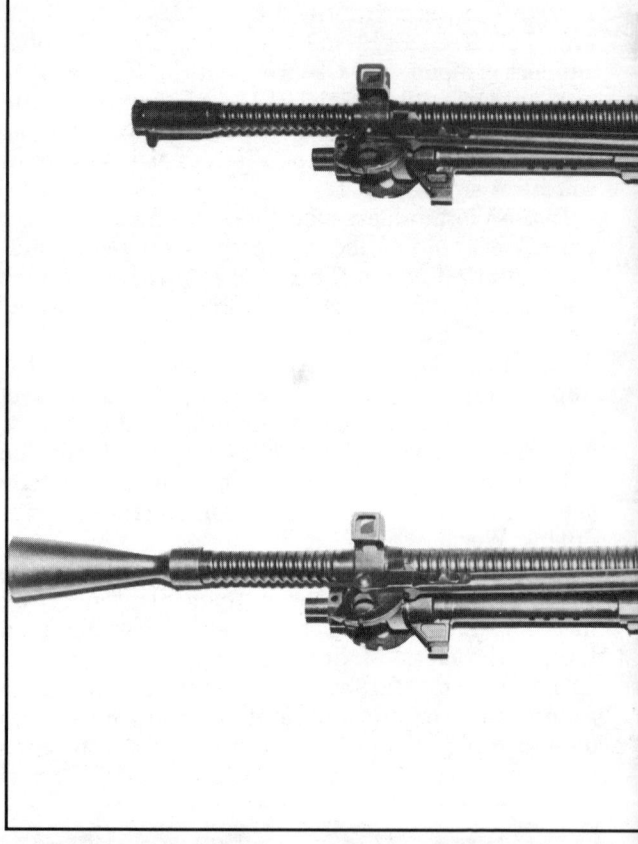

compatibility between rifle and machine gun ammunition, right down to clips. In practice standard rifle cartridges battered the Type 11's operating mechanism. Hence a special reduced power cartridge was supposed to be employed in Type 11 light machine guns. Insufficient supplies of this special ammunition reached the Vietminh, largely due to poor logistic support, and this may have limited their use of these light machine guns.

The 7.7 × 57mm Type 99 (1939) light machine gun, which was created by the Japanese to replace the Type 11, had been a considerable technical step forward. The Japanese had decided in 1932 to re-equip their army with this gun, based on a Czechoslovakian (ZB-36) pattern machine gun used by the

Chinese Nationalist Army, because it fired the 7.7mm cartridge. The resulting weapon was a good one, and it became a favorite of Vietminh troops.

The Japanese 7.7 × 57mm Type 92 (1932) heavy machine gun was a slightly modernized version of the 6.5mm Type 3 that had first appeared in 1914. Both were copies of the French Hotchkiss the Japanese had adopted in 1905. It was very heavy (55.4 kg with tripod), but the gun and tripod had been designed so that they could be carried cross-country by three men. The Type 92 was a very reliable and rugged weapon that was capable of delivering accurate long-range supporting fire. It was phased out of service in favor of lighter Soviet and Chinese machine guns.

Aid for the ARVN

4

Small arms of the American advisory years, 1954-65

AFTER THE GENEVA AGREEMENT of 1954 partitioned Vietnam along the 17th Parallel into the North and South, the new governments set about organizing their armed forces. The North Vietnamese Army (NVA) looked to Soviet and Chinese sources for its organizational structure and for equipment assistance. The armed forces of South Vietnam looked to the United States for guidance and materiel support. While the North Vietnamese Army was basically a coherent fighting organization from the outset (it was a reworking of Vietminh forces) with a clear-cut political ideology, the Army of the Republic of Vietnam (ARVN) proved more difficult to organize, because the South Vietnamese military and political goals were less coherently defined.

At the outset of the North-South conflict, the Vietminh had over 230,000 veteran fighters (nine infantry divisions and two artillery divisions) and 100,000 "Armed People's Militia." Many Vietminh troops went north following the partition, but an estimated 50,000 cadres remained in the South. In contrast the South Vietnamese National Army had a nominal paper strength of about 150,000 men plus 35,000 auxiliaries. However, since most of its 125 battalions were understrength, the National Army's effective fighters numbered between 65,000 and 70,000. The authorized strength of the South's Civil Guard, activated in April 1955, was 68,000 and the authorized strength of the People's Militia, activated in April 1956, was 48,000. This force was equipped with a mixture of Japanese, French, and American weapons. Increasingly, as time passed the standard infantry rifles became the .30 caliber (7.62 × 63mm) M-1 (Garand) semiautomatic rifle and the .30 caliber

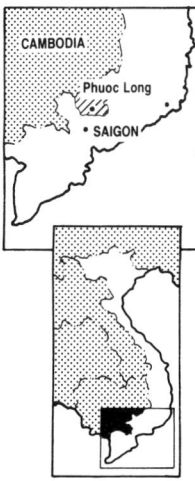

Aid for the ARVN

OVERSIZE: The general consensus about the US .30 cal. M-1 Garand rifle was that it was too large for the Vietnamese. The size and power of the weapon was tailored to the stature of the average American infantryman. Very early in the advisory period, the American and ARVN commanders agreed that a smaller and more suitable weapon was needed for the smaller Vietnamese.

(7.62 × 33mm) M-1 and M-2 carbines, neither of which was suited for combat in Vietnam or to the needs of the Vietnamese infantryman.

These American shoulder weapons continued to be the basic weapons of the new Army of the Republic of Vietnam (ARVN), which came into being following the establishment of the Republic of Vietnam on 26 October 1955. During the years 1957-58 the basic goal of the ARVN logistics service was standardization with American military equipment, according to Lieutenant General Dong Van Khuyen, the last Chief of Staff of the Joint General Staff of the Republic of Vietnam Armed

Grease gun —The compact and easy to carry US .45 cal. M-3 submachine gun, "grease gun," was a favorite ARVN patrol weapon. Its major shortcoming was its lack of killing power at ranges greater than 100 meters.

Forces, who helped build the RVNAF logistic system. By standardizing equipment many supply problems could be simplified and the eclectic mixture of older French and Japanese weapons could be scrapped.

With the help of Lieutenant General John W. O'Daniel, the South Vietnamese created two new types of divisions, establishing four field and six light divisions. The light division (5,225 men) was about one-third the size of a standard US infantry division, and was intended to be a small "mobile striking force unencumbered by unnecessary equipment but with considerable firepower for

In enemy hands —A Viet Cong fighter from the Cu Chi region stands armed with a US .30 cal. M-1 rifle. Note both its size in comparison to his height, and the 8-shot clip of ammunition affixed to the rifle's sling.

close-in fighting." Created for action in the jungles, paddies, and mountains where roads were nonexistent, it had 30 percent more light machine guns than an American division, 10 percent more Browning automatic rifles, and the same number of 60mm and 81mm mortars. The Vietnamese light division had no organic artillery, ordnance, or quartermaster support units. Additionally, the amount of transportation equipment was much smaller than that of a comparable American unit. The South Vietnamese field divisions had 8,500 men and included a 105mm howitzer battalion, as well as engineer, signal, quartermaster, ordnance, transportation, and intelligence companies.

These new style ARVN divisions were generally supported by the small amount of American-made armor available—most of which had been left behind by the French. An ARVN armored regiment was deployed in each of the four military districts, with each regiment being equipped with M-8 Greyhound armored cars, M-3 half-tracks, M-3 scout cars,and towed 75mm howitzers. This armored force was later strengthened by grants-in-aid from the US Military Assistance program.

In addition to the light and field divisions, there were 13 territorial regiments for regional security. These latter units, if the need arose, could be consolidated into three more light divisions. Well into 1956, most of these ARVN fighting formations existed only on paper. The 1st Field Division was the only division with real fighting capacity and firepower. Building the South Vietnamese into a genuine fighting force took several years.

For nearly three years after the 1954 partition, an uneasy truce existed between the two parts of Vietnam, while they tried to consolidate control in their respective territories. During 1954-57 the communist cadres in the South completed their own organization; establishing caches of weapons and ammunition, setting up operations bases, organizing intelligence gathering networks, and training men in guerrilla warfare. These communist cadres came to be known as the Viet Cong, although their formal name was the Viet Nam Cong San (National Front for the Liberation of South Vietnam).

In 1957, responding to closer ties between the Republic of Vietnam and the United States, Le Duan

HALFWAY CHOICE: An ARVN soldier, armed with a .30 cal. M-1 semiautomatic carbine, takes up a defensive position at a Self Defense Force Outpost at Ly Van Manh in January 1963. The .30 M-1 carbine was smaller than the M-1 rifle, but it was much less powerful. A weapon midway between the two in size and lethality was needed.

(1908-1986), then the senior Viet Cong leader, traveled to Hanoi to confer with the North Vietnamese leadership and to receive his orders. After he returned to the South, 6,000 VC fighters began guerrilla activities against the South Vietnamese government. By year's end, 400 minor local South Vietnamese political leaders had been assassinated by the Viet Cong. Between 1959 and 1961, the number of South Vietnamese government officials killed increased from 1,200 to 4,000 a year. In that same two-year period, between 1,800 and 2,700 additional fighters entered South Vietnam from the North, bringing with them their basic weapons and initial allotments of ammunition. The United States responded by activating the US Army's 1st Special Forces Group in Okinawa. American Green Berets were soon engaged in training Vietnamese Special Forces at Nha Trang.

Aid for the ARVN

HOME GUARD: A rice farmer in a hamlet in the Delta, who served as a squad leader in the South Vietnamese People's Self-Defense Forces, faces the camera armed with a .45 cal. M-1A1 Thompson submachine gun while his companion keeps guard with a .30 cal. M-1 carbine. On average only one man in five in a self-defense unit had a weapon available to him.

Simultaneously, military supplies soon began reaching the Viet Cong forces in the South via the jungle route that had been hacked out of the triple canopy jungle of neighboring Laos by North Vietnamese logistic units such as Groups 559 and 759. The Ho Chi Minh Trail rapidly became the principal source of weapons and reinforcements for forces operating against the ARVN. By 1961, the Viet Cong military activity throughout South Vietnam had escalated into a running war, averaging 600 incidents a month.

Criticism of the South Vietnamese government

of President Ngo Dinh Diem (1901-1963) grew because of its inability to end or at least contain guerrilla activities. By mid-September 1961 the Viet Cong felt sufficiently powerful to launch a 1,500-man attack against the Phuoc Long provincial capital, Phuoc Vinh, a mere 60 kilometers north of Saigon. They successfully overwhelmed the local garrison and publicly executed the provincial governor. The ARVN counterattacked and retook the town on the following day. But the Viet Cong gained political credibility, and the Diem government lost political points. As an aftermath

of this defeat, Diem finally agreed to a major increase in American military aid and advisers. More significantly, he accepted the employment of US support forces. The first of these, two H-21C helicopter transport companies, arrived in December.

As the Military Assistance Command Vietnam (MACV) began a program of instruction and re-equipment, the ARVN ability to maneuver about the countryside improved rapidly. By the end of 1962, 11,000 American advisory and support personnel were in the field alongside more than 500,000 ARVN troops. Civil turmoil and political instability occupied the South Vietnamese government during the early 1960s, preventing the combined ARVN and American forces from effectively countering the growing enemy threat.

Despite the South's political instability, the Americans continued to deliver new types of military materiel. For example, the M-113 armored personnel carriers (APCs) gave new mobility to the ARVN infantry units. In April 1962 enough M-113s to equip two companies were delivered to the 7th and 21st ARVN Infantry Divisions. Many problems were experienced with training these first armored infantry units (derived largely from the ARVN commanders' limited armored warfare experience

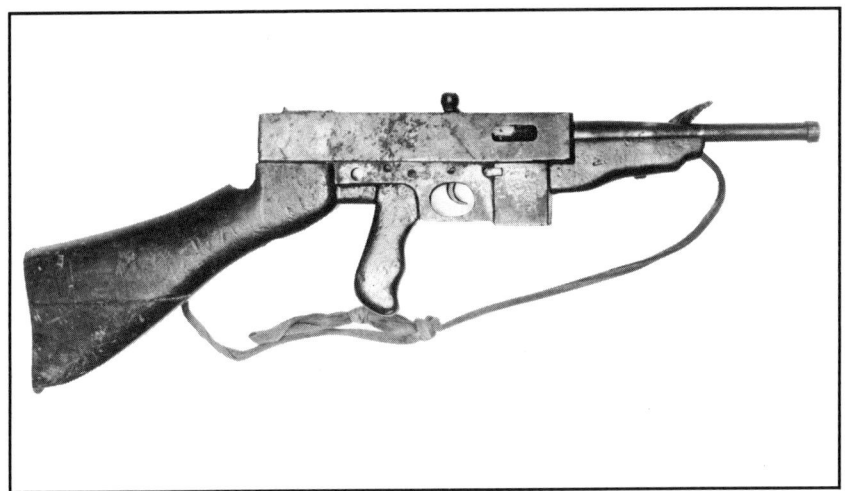

and their disinclination to listen to their US advisers). Still, the M-113 APC proved to be a very useful vehicle.

The M-113 was originally developed by the US Army as a protected personnel carrier, but it came to be used as a light tank by the ARVN. Lightly protected with aluminum armor, and carrying a flexible .50 caliber (12.7 × 99mm) M-2 Browning heavy machine gun mounted on the roof, the M-113 had room for 11 infantrymen, plus the driver and a machine gunner. Its tracks gave it excellent cross-country mobility, it could swim rivers and canals when necessary, and it was practically the only combat vehicle that could cope with muddy or flooded rice paddies. At this early phase of the war the Viet Cong had a limited number of weapons that could stop these APCs.

The initial successes of the two ARVN armored infantry units led to more M-113s being sent to South Vietnam by the United States. Additionally, the newly developed M-114 command and reconnaissance vehicle was sent to the war zone. By the middle of 1963, each of the four ARVN armored regiments had one squadron of M-24 Chafee light tanks, one squadron of M-8 armored cars, one squadron of M-114s, and two mechanized rifle squadrons with M-113s. The latter units were similar in structure to the earlier mechanized rifle companies, but carried more firepower. The mechanized rifle squadrons each had three M-1 81mm mortars and one M-18A1 57mm recoilless rifle. Meanwhile, large quantities of munitions were still being shipped to the North Vietnamese Army. In 1962 alone, if Chinese accounts are to be believed, they provided a combined total of 90,000 rifles and machine guns to the NVA.

Late in 1963, following the coup that deposed and killed President Diem, American aid to the new South Vietnamese government was increased, as was direct US military assistance such as intensified aerial bombing and naval gun fire support. But the ground battles continued to run in favor of the Viet Cong, and by 1965, they controlled large portions of the rural areas of South Vietnam. The VC were gradually encroaching on Saigon and other major cities. The American government decided on direct intervention with US ground troops when some 6,000 Viet Cong moved within striking distance of the principal US air base at Da Nang.

The United States materiel support of the South

THE SPECIALS' SPECIALS: A South Vietnamese soldier (top) on guard duty at dawn armed with a 9 × 19mm Swedish "K" (Carl Gustav) submachine gun. The weapon was very popular with Special Forces and other special operations units. A South Vietnamese soldier (below) stands watch armed with a US .30 cal. (7.62 × 63mm) Browning automatic rifle. The weapon was popular as a squad automatic weapon during the advisory period.

Vietnamese had become substantial. By the end of 1964, in small arms alone, the Americans had delivered 124,732 .30 caliber (7.62 × 63mm) M-1 rifles; 344,382 .30 caliber (7.62 × 33mm) M-1 carbines; and 2,334 .30 caliber (7.62 × 33mm) M-2 carbines to the ARVN. These basic weapons were supplemented by a handful of .45 caliber (11.43 × 23mm) M-3-type submachine guns (127 before 1965); 4,685 .30 caliber (7.62 × 63mm) M-1918A2 Browning automatic rifles; and 6,770 .30 caliber (7.62 × 63mm) light machine guns (mostly M-1919A4s). These weapons were provided to the ARVN to counter a concurrent weapons modernization program that was taking place in enemy units.

For local defense forces, the United States delivered more than 54,000 12-gauge combat-type shotguns (Savages, Ithacas, Winchesters, and Remingtons) before 1965. In addition, the American government provided 23,000 handguns, all but 2,100 of which were .45 caliber M-1911A1-type, for officers and NCOs throughout the ARVN and local defense forces. Infantry fire support was provided by American-made 60mm, 80mm, and 4.2-inch mortars, while the standard artillery piece was the US 105mm M-1 howitzer. Of these fire support weapons, nearly 2,700 were 60mm mortars.

HEAVY LIGHTWEIGHT:
A Vietnamese machine gunner rests his 13.7 kg US .30 cal. M-1919A6 "light" machine gun on a tree stump while searching for Viet Cong. As with other US weapons these Browning machine guns were too heavy to be considered useful for long-distance patrolling. The M-1919A6 was replaced by the 9.4 kg 7.62mm NATO US M-60 machine gun.

The blooding of the M-16

Small arms of the American combat years: 1965-73

AMERICAN COMBAT FORCES were committed reluctantly to the war in 1965. US Marine Corps combat elements of the Third Marine Regiment, Third Marine Division, were assigned to protect the Da Nang air base on 6 March 1965. The US Army's 173rd Airborne Brigade arrived in Vietnam on 5 May. By July, American personnel in South Vietnam numbered more than 50,000. New military hardware accompanied the Americans. Most of these troops arrived with their 7.62mm caliber NATO M-14 rifles and M-60 machine guns as basic weapons. Both weapons had been adopted in 1957 as part of the post-1945 modernization of US infantry weapons.

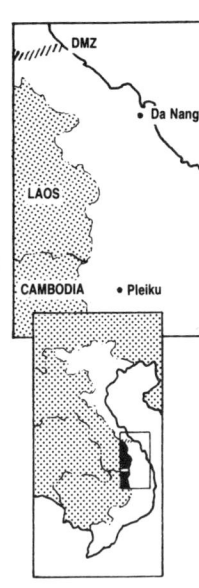

On the opposing side, after having infiltrated between 20,000 and 37,000 men into the South between 1959 and 1965, the government in the North decided to introduce regular forces of the People's Army of Vietnam (PAVN), the official name of the North Vietnamese ground force, into the conflict. This decision led to changes in the materiel used against both ARVN and American troops. The first PAVN (or NVA as they were called in the South) regulars had moved down the Ho Chi Minh Trail in April 1964. By year's end more than 10,000 NVA troops made that trek. This was a small number when compared to later years when as many as 22,000 northerners would move southward each month. All of these fighters brought their own weapons and initial loads of ammunition with them. The seesaw escalation upward of allied and enemy

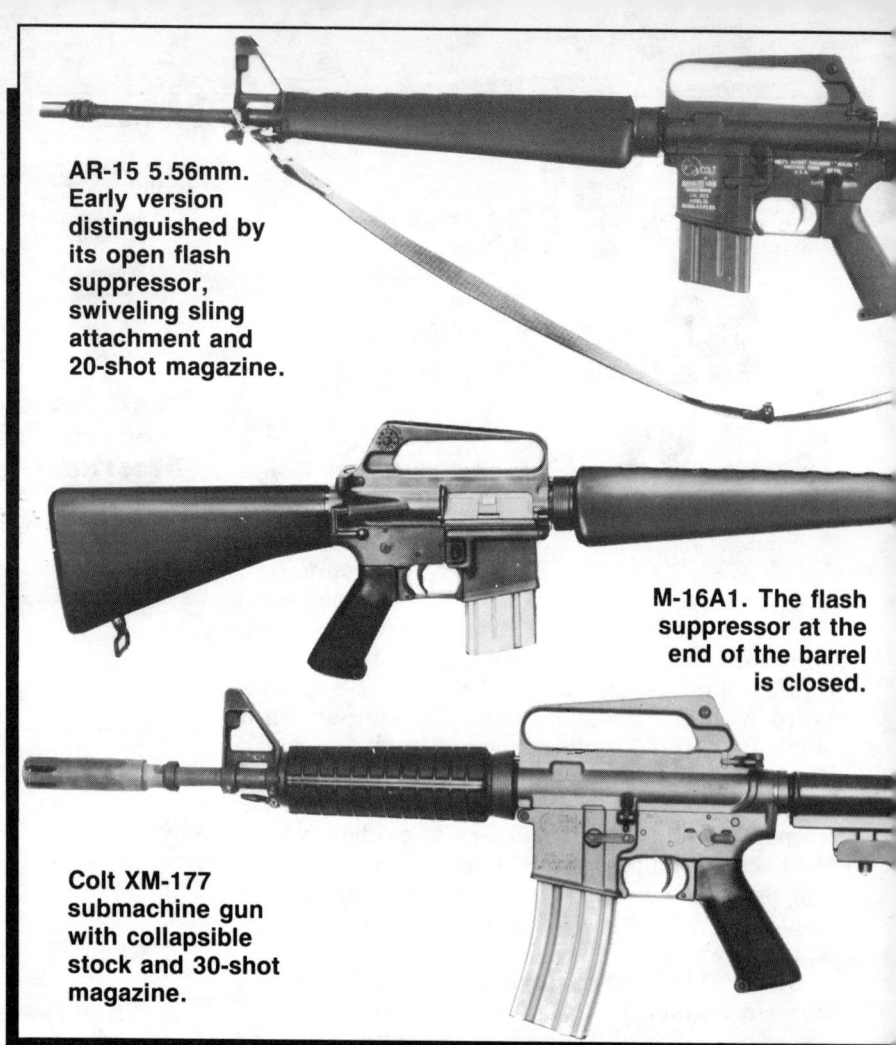

AR-15 5.56mm. Early version distinguished by its open flash suppressor, swiveling sling attachment and 20-shot magazine.

M-16A1. The flash suppressor at the end of the barrel is closed.

Colt XM-177 submachine gun with collapsible stock and 30-shot magazine.

military forces brought continued infusions of weapons and munitions.

When it came to the personal weapons of the infantryman, the Vietnam War was a watershed for small arms design. Perhaps the most significant result of the Vietnam War was the impetus the conflict gave to the adoption of the small caliber assault rifle. The Indochinese battlefield experience ultimately led internationally to the 1980s re-equipment of most major armies with either 5.56mm or 5.45mm rifles.

After the establishment of the North Atlantic

WORKHORSE AND SCAPEGOAT

Colt's 5.56mm (.223 cal.) AR-15 was the first in a series of rifles that became the M-16 family. By the end of 1969 it was the basic shoulder weapon for American, South Vietnamese, Korean, Australian and other forces.

Cursed at, and praised, the M-16s were controversial from the start. Troops either loved them or they hated them. Few were neutral in their opinions about the lightweight "Black Rifle."

The very first AR-15s sent to Vietnam had dark olive greenstocks. The color was later changed to black, hence the weapon's nickname. When emergency steps were taken in 1968-69 to remedy problems encountered in combat, some significant changes were made to the weapon. Modifications incorporated into the design that became the M-16A1 included a butt storage compartment and trapdoor for cleaning accessories, a fixed position rear slingswivel, forward assist plunger for the bolt, and an enclosed flash suppressor. Where the AR-15/M-16 rifles had bright chrome-plated bolt assemblies, the M-16A1s had dull phosphated bolts and bolt carriers. Later M-16 rifles used by the US Air Force looked much like the M-16A1 with the absence of the forward assist plunger. The XM-177 "Commando" (CAR-15) submachine gun was a shortened version of the M-16A1 with a retractable stock assembly and a special muzzle device to reduce blast, flash, and noise.

Treaty Organization (1949) the US Army had pushed for creation of lighter weight rifles and more portable, general purpose machine guns (GPMG). The resulting US weapons were the M-14 rifle and the M-60 machine gun, both of which fired the standard 7.62 × 51mm NATO cartridge. The American M-14 rifle was essentially a product improved M-1 Garand that had a 20-round magazine and which fired the shortened NATO cartridge. Other NATO countries adopted other 7.62mm caliber NATO rifles and GPMGs.

In the East, the Soviet Union had introduced their

Early version —An ARVN soldier conducts a search in the Mekong Delta armed with an early version of the 5.56 × 45mm AR-15 rifle. This was one of the first 1,000 AR-15 rifles sent to Vietnam by the Advanced Research Projects Agency for evaluation. These first AR-15s had an open prong flash suppressor and a leather grip on the bayonet.

7.62 × 39mm caliber weapons that included the AK-47 assault rifle, the SKS carbine, and the RPD light machine gun. Nearly simultaneous with the US Army adoption of the M-14 rifle, experiments were started to evolve a still smaller and lighter weapon that would be effective at ranges up to about 400 meters. Battlefield analysis had shown 400 meters was the maximum combat rifle range for about 95 percent of infantry shooting.

This analytical work led Eugene M. Stoner and his colleagues at the Armalite Company in Costa Mesa, California, to develop the AR-15 rifle. This weapon fired a .223 caliber bullet (5.56mm) at a comparatively high velocity of 990 meters per second (m/s). Tests of the initial AR-15 design in 1958 were followed by some minor modifications and a recommendation that the 5.56mm AR-15 rifle be considered as a replacement for the 7.62mm M-14 rifle. That proposed process was speeded up by the activities of the Department of Defense's Advanced Research Projects Agency (ARPA), a section charged with implementing new projects. In the summer of 1962, ARPA sent 1,000 AR-15s to Vietnam for evaluation by South Vietnamese troops.

Combat use had demonstrated that the smaller stature Vietnamese troops found American rifles such as the 4.3 kg, 1.11-meter long .30 caliber (7.62 × 63mm) M-1 rifle very difficult to shoot and carry. The lighter .30 caliber (7.62 × 33mm) M-1 and M-2 carbines were very popular, but much less effective as combat weapons due to the lower power of their cartridge. The 5.56 × 45mm AR-15 promised greater firepower in a lighter and more manageable package. Typical of the comments received from the field were the following remarks from the American adviser accompanying a platoon from the ARVN 340 Ranger Company:

> On 16 June . . . (we) contacted three armed VC in heavily forested jungle. Two VC had carbines, grenades, mines, and one had a SMG. At a distance of approximately 15 meters, one Ranger fired an AR-15 full automatic hitting one VC with three rounds with the first burst. One round in the head took it completely off. Another in the right arm, took it completely off too. One round hit him in the right side, causing a hole about five inches in diameter

.... it can be assumed that any one of the three wounds would have caused death.

Reports such as this one led to the ultimate decision to provide more AR-15 (later renamed M-16) rifles on an experimental basis to the ARVN. In mid-1963, the Department of Defense ordered 85,000 AR-15s for the Army and 19,000 for the US Air Force from Colt Firearms. This first contract was later expanded to provide 116,695 M-16 rifles and 84,350 M-16A1s. Deliveries of these guns began in March 1964 and were completed by the end of September 1966. The second contract to Colt was for 836,810 rifles, all of which were delivered by February 1969.

Despite the fact that the M-16 (AR-15) had been viewed at the start as a weapon for the Vietnamese, American troops were the first to receive this rifle. When the first US Marines arrived in Da Nang to protect the air base on 6 March 1965, they had exchanged their 7.62mm NATO M-14 rifles for the new 5.56mm rifle. The men of the 173d Airborne Brigade, the first Army fighting unit sent to Vietnam in May 1965, were also issued the M-16 rifle.

Marine variant —A Marine carries a 7.62mm M-14 rifle during a village search in the autumn of 1965. Later the Marines received the 5.56mm M-16 rifle.

As the American soldiers and Marines began to fight equipped with the M-16 rifle, General William C. Westmoreland, Commander of the US Military Assistance Command,Vietnam, (MACV), called for reports about its suitability in battle. In the Ia Drang Valley battle of November 1965, troops of the 7th Cavalry Regiment fought a fierce fight against North Vietnamese regulars. In the words of Lieutenant Colonel Harold G. Moore, Jr., commander of the 1st Battalion of the 7th, "brave soldiers and the M-16 brought" about the allied victory. Moore and his colleagues told General Westmoreland that the M-16 was the best individual infantry weapon ever made. It was seen as the weapon to counter the enemy's AK-47 assault rifles. Accepting the endorsement of his frontline fighters, the MACV commander asked Secretary of Defense Robert S. McNamara "as a matter of urgency to equip all American forces with the M-16 and then also to equip the ARVN with it."

In the fall of 1965, General Westmoreland informed the South Vietnamese Joint General Staff that an emergency request for 170,000 (later

The blooding of the M-16

SIXTEENS ON PARADE: A group of ARVN and 101st Airborne troops, about to board helicopters for a mission into VC-held territory, display some of the different configurations of the M-16-type weapons in service in Vietnam. The ARVN soldier on the far left has an XM-16E1 with an open flash suppressor, the American wearing sunglasses has an M-16A1 with the improved closed suppressor, and the soldier immediately behind him to the right has an M-16 with a very early pronged flash suppressor.

adjusted downward to 100,000) M-16 rifles had been sent to the US Department of Defense. But defense officials at the Pentagon downgraded the urgent priority Westmoreland had assigned to providing M-16 rifles. It was not until 1967 that there were enough M-16s for all American combat troops—maneuver units, as they were known—to receive the M-16. ARVN troops waited until the next year. In Westmoreland's opinion, the ARVN "thus long fought at a serious disadvantage against the enemy's automatic AK-47, armed as they were with World War II's semiautomatic M-1."

As American troops began to use the M-16, there were renewed requests from the Vietnamese for this automatic weapon. Lieutenant General Dong Van Khuyen, the former ARVN Chief of Staff, recalls the

excitement generated by the news that ARVN troops were about to receive the M-16:

"Every combat unit longed for the day the M-16 arrived in country. The M-16 did arrive finally but in the hands of US combat troops because the buildup of US forces in South Vietnam had pre-empted all priorities for RVNAF equipment. The decision to postpone delivery of the M-16 stemmed from the fact that, by mutual agreement, the RVNAF were to assume the lesser role of supporting pacification against local enemy forces while US units conducted search-and-destroy operations against enemy main forces. The ARVN desire for the M-16 persisted, however; it was perhaps more ardent now than ever, now that even enemy local forces (VC) were uniformly equipped with the AK-47."

RIVAL SELF-LOADERS: Members of the 1st Battalion, Royal Australian Regiment, armed with a 7.62mm M-60 machine gun and 7.62mm NATO SLRs (L1A1) take up a defensive position around the Bien Hoa air base in June 1966. The self-loading L1A1 was a Belgian design weapon (FN-FAL). In prototype form, it had competed with the US M-14 rifle for adoption by the US Army.

In the spring of 1967, the first 100,000 M-16 rifles earmarked for the ARVN began to arrive. By year's end, enough of the new rifles had arrived to equip the ARVN airborne and marine battalions. Still there was a continuing debate between MACV Headquarters and the Pentagon about the pace at which the remaining ARVN units should receive M-16 rifles.

The 1968 Tet General Offensive by the northern forces ended the debate. For the first time the concentrated firepower impact of enemy troops equipped with the selective fire AK-47 was fully felt. MACV struggled around the clock with an emergency airlift of M-16 rifles to ARVN troops in Saigon and Da Nang. Crash training courses were held to familiarize ARVN personnel with the new rifle. In rapid succession, all South Vietnamese infantry battalions in III, I, IV, and II Corps, as well as Ranger units, received their M-16s. This rifle change-over was completed by mid-1968. The speed with which the US and ARVN authorities moved to place the M-16 in the hands of the ARVN combat soldiers stunned the enemy. When the NVA and VC initiated the second phase of their planned offensive in Quang Ngai Province, they were caught completely off guard and overwhelmed by the deadly combined individual firepower put up by the defenders of the ARVN 2d Division. That unit had received its M-16 rifles only 24 hours earlier. In fact, several battalions had not even had time to adjust the sights of their new rifles.

By the end of 1968, both the US military forces and those of the ARVN made the transition from the older generation of .30 caliber (7.62 × 63mm) and 7.62 × 51mm NATO caliber weapons to the new generation of 5.56 × 45mm rifles. By the end of 1968, the South Vietnamese military forces had been provided with just over 600,000 M-16-type rifles. By the end of the war in April 1975, the United States government had shipped 943,989 M-16 and M-16A1 rifles for the ARVN.

By the end of 1969, the ARVN infantry battalions had also received 7.62mm NATO caliber M-60 general purpose machine guns to replace their older .30 caliber BARs and M-1919A4 light machine guns. Their firepower was further reinforced with new issues of the M-79 40mm grenade launchers,

ID PARADE:
This photograph of a 7.62 × 39mm Hungarian AMD-65 rifle, a folding stock version of the AK-M rifle, was issued by the Combat Materiel Exploitation Center (CMEC) to frontline troops. CMEC's full-time job was identifying new enemy hardware, evaluating its combat significance, and then issuing intelligence bulletins about it to the men in the field.

M-72 Light Antitank Weapon (LAW), and the M-67 90mm recoilless rifle, all of which proved extremely effective against enemy fortified emplacements and personnel caught out in the open. By the end of 1968, the new family of weapons had placed the ARVN on a equal firepower footing with US infantry units.

However, the debut of the 5.56mm M-16-type weapons was marred by operational problems in combat with the weapon. Many of these were caused by insufficient maintenance of the weapon—a result of early public relations claims that the M-16 did not require as much routine cleaning as other rifles. Unfortunately some troops accepted this sales hype as an excuse for not properly maintaining their rifles. US Army Ordnance officials encouraged this slothfulness by failing to issue cleaning equipment with the new rifles. This inattention to good housekeeping led to a rash of functional problems; failures to extract, failures to eject, failures to feed, and other mysterious stoppages. Irate letters from troops in the field soon found their way stateside.

Representative James J. Howard, of New Jersey, opened the controversy when he reprinted a letter sent home by a Marine who charged that the M-16 was unreliable and deadly to his compatriots in the

field. Such an expressive letter could not be ignored:

I just got your letter today aboard ship. We've been on an operation ever since the 21st of last month. I can just see the papers back home now—enemy casualties heavy, Marine casualties light. Let me give you some statistics and you decide if they were light. We left with close to 1,400 men in our battalion and came back with half. We left with 250 men in our company and came back with 107. We left with

MAINTENANCE IS THE MESSAGE: The cover of an official comic-style manual persuading troops to take care of their M-16 series weapons.

The blooding of the M-16

PUTTING IT OVER:

In 1968, the Department of Defense had no hesitation in employing a Jane-type figure to put its message over. But if the tone of the 32-page pamphlet about care and maintenance of the M-16A1 was unashamedly sexist, it was also effective. The M-16A1 was not beset by any of the controversies surrounding its predecessor, the M-16.

TIPS THAT'LL KEEP IT YOUR EVER-LOVIN...

SWEET 16

Here're a few cleaning and operati
tips that'll help you get best resu
from your weapon. Some of these ti
sort of put the accent on stuff you
find in the rifle's bible—TM 9-100
249-12 (1968). Others are hex
and fixes direct from guys who've be
living with this light-weight terror.

8

72 men in our platoon and came back with 19. I knew I was pressing my luck. They finally got me. It wasn't bad though, I just caught a little shrapnel. I would say the same for all my buddies. ... believe it or not, you know what killed most of us? Our own rifle. Before we left Okinawa, (we) were all issued this new rifle, the M-16. Practically everyone of our dead was found with his rifle torn down next to him where he had been trying to fix it. There was a newspaper woman with us photographing all this and the Pentagon found out about it and won't let her publish the pictures. They say that they don't want to get the American people upset. Isn't that a laugh?

TIP...

For instance, with the Joe in a position to know, it's the new-type aluminum magazine umpteen hundred to 0 over the steel-type that came with the early models. The steel mags sometimes caused bolt lock failure and failure to feed.

So, if you have the steel type, turn it in pronto for the aluminum one. They both take the same stock number

STEER CLEAR OF IT.

THIS ONE'S OK.

—FSN 1005-056-2237—but they're easy to tell apart. The one you want has three vertical ribs, while the one you want to steer clear of has crossed and vertical ribs.

TIP...

Speaking of magazines . . . every guy has his own idea of how firm or loose he wants the holding action of the magazine catch to be. Which is A-OK as far as it goes. But remember this: The tighter the mag's held in the receiver, the more pressure it takes to release it. And this: The farther the shaft of the catch sticks through the catch button, the tighter the magazine's held in the receiver.

RELEASE MAGAZINE.

MAGAZINE CATCH BUTTON.

9

Initially, the US military categorically denied reports of M-16 rifle unreliability. Marine General Lewis Walt stated from his headquarters in Vietnam that his troops unanimously favored the new M-16. He quoted a captain whose company had captured the strategically important Hill 881 overlooking the isolated Khe Sanh combat base to the effect that "we couldn't have taken the hill without it." General Wallace M. Greene, Jr., Commandant of the Marine Corps, held a special press conference "to correct the faulty impression that some people seem to have that the Marine Corps is dissatisfied with this weapon." General Greene said that the tales were nonsense, and he contended that the M-16 had "proved to be a real hard hitting, lightweight rifle ideally suited to the jungle type of environment in Vietnam." Marine Corps brass were happy with the M-16.

The subcommittee established by the US House of Representatives to investigate reported problems with the weapon did not share the Marine Corps' enthusiastic opinion of the M-16. Shortly after starting their review of the rifle program, subcommittee members witnessed the weapon malfunction in demonstration firings at Fort Benning and Camp Pendleton. In view of the conflicting claims made by the officers and combat troops, members of the committee went to Vietnam. Following their trip, the members of the subcommittee concluded that there were flaws in the rifle/ammunition mix that were due to the lack of proper US Army management of the rifle's procurement.

The subcommittee's words were harsh. "The much-troubled M-16 rifle is basically an excellent weapon whose problems were largely caused by Army mismanagement." Subcommittee members decided that the rifle program had been operated in the most "unbelievable" manner. "The existing command structure was either inadequate or inoperative." Moreover, inquiries indicated that the way the system worked made "it almost impossible to pinpoint responsibility when mistakes are made." There was "substantial evidence of lack of activity on the part of responsible officials of the highest authority even when the problems of the M-16 and its ammunition came to their attention." These bleak observations forced the subcommittee to conclude "that under the present system problems are too slowly recognized and reactions to problems are even slower."

In the course of the Congressional investigation four major factors were discovered that contributed to the poor performance of the M-16. These were the use of a high-residue ball-type propellant powder; the failure of the Army to require a chromium plated barrel and chamber; the lack of proper lubricants and cleaning equipment; and the failure to properly familiarize the troops with the maintenance needs of the weapon. All of these problems could have been eliminated with coordinated planning and

PUTTING MAGGIE TOGETHER

Here's the easy way . . . gently:

1. Nose the bullet end of the follower into the body at a 45-degree angle till it touches the inside edge of the body.

2. Work the other end of the follower into the body.

3. Just wiggle the spring into the mag as far as it'll go.

4. Make sure the printing on the floor plate is on the outside. Slide the plate in this way, then press the spring down with your thumb. And make sure the floor plate goes under all 4 tabs, too.

HERE'S AN IMPORTANT **TIP:** IF THE SPRING SHOULD ACCIDENTALLY GET SEPARATED FROM THE FOLLOWER, TURN THE MAGAZINE OVER TO YOUR ARMORER! **DON'T** TRY TO FIX IT YOURSELF. LOOKS EASY, SURE, BUT WITHOUT THE RIGHT TOOL YOU'D DAMAGE THE SPRING... AND END UP WITH FEEDING TROUBLE.

27

supervision. Each of these problems was tackled by the US Army Weapons Command personnel, and solutions were found. To compensate for the use of ball-type propellant, the cartridge chamber and barrel were chrome plated; the buffer assembly was redesigned; and the troops were issued proper cleaning equipment and bombarded with a massive educational program about proper weapon maintenance.

Once the changes were made, the M-16 rifle

became a very popular weapon with US, ARVN, and allied infantrymen. Debate would continue about the relative effectiveness of the 5.56mm bullet and the 7.62mm NATO projectile, but once redeemed the M-16 family went on to become one of the most significant battle rifles of the 20th century. Overhauled and product improved in the early 1980s, and called the M-16A2, this weapon remains the standard rifle of the US infantryman at the end of the 1980s.

For those who keep track of milestones, the US Air Force adopted the 5.56mm M-16 as their standard rifle on 8 February 1964. At that same time the XM-16E1 rifle, with its forward bolt assist, became limited standard for the US Army. Three years later on 28 February 1967 that latter weapon became the M-16A1 rifle. Ultimately it became the basic rifle for the US Army.

During the mid-to-late 1960s, the US Army evaluated a number of weapons Colt engineers evolved from the basic AR-15/M-16 design. The most significant of these variants was the CAR-15, a carbine/submachine gun version of the basic rifle. The first of these, with a 254mm barrel and collapsible sliding stock, were built in 1965. Experiments soon followed in the combat zones of Vietnam, resulting in a brief study of this weapon in November 1965 by the operations (G-3) staff of the US Army Vietnam (USARV). The USARV study of the CAR-15 "Commando" suggested the desirability of replacing certain weapons with this shortened rifle. The USARV report suggested that:

Lube thoroughly —White-gloves inspections were ruled out for fear that troops might be tempted to give their M-16s a bath beforehand and wash away all the LSA weapons oil. An M-16 used in combat required cleaning and oiling three to five times a day.

1. The calibers .45 and .38 pistols and the M-3 SMG should be replaced by the CAR-15 because its range, firepower, and automatic capability should be significantly better than those other weapons.
2. The M-16 rifle should be replaced by the easier to handle and carry CAR-15 for those personnel who needed to keep their hands free for other duties.
3. The employment of the CAR-15 would improve the combat capability of USARV through increased firepower.

To evaluate the combat potential of the CAR-15, the US Army established an ENSURE (Expediting

M16A1 SHARPSHOOTERS,
MAKE THIS YOUR SOP...

DRAIN BEFORE SHOOTING

No sweat, y'say, getting rid of a barrelful of water after fording a stream or rice paddy? Just point the muzzle down and let it drain, y'say?

Don't bet your life on it! Not with a rifle with a bore as small as the M16A1's.

Here's why: Surface tension of the water and capillary traction in a small area like this makes it hard to get water out. If enough stays in there and you fire off — Bang! There goes another barrel — and maybe a chunk of you.

Water could triple the pressure in the bore when the weapon's fired.

So, make this your own personal SOP every time you drag out of the drink or fight in a heavy rain in Charleyland. Before you fire that weapon:

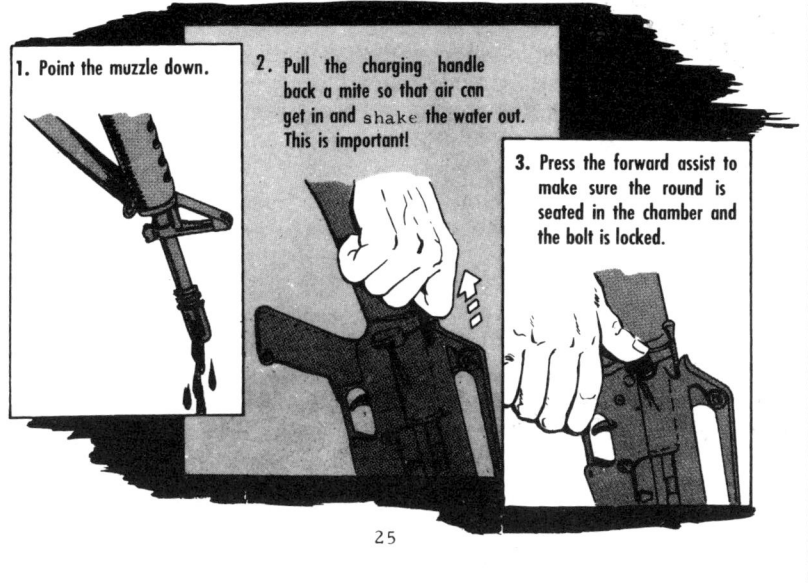

1. Point the muzzle down.

2. Pull the charging handle back a mite so that air can get in and shake the water out. This is important!

3. Press the forward assist to make sure the round is seated in the chamber and the bolt is locked.

25

One of the insignia of the 5th Special Forces Group —The 5th SOG was one of several elite units to endorse the CAR-15.

Non-Standard Urgent Requirements for Equipment) project to acquire 2,800 of these weapons.

The Army Concept Team In Vietnam (ACTIV) was assigned the task of testing the CAR-15 for combat effectiveness and suitability as a military weapon. ACTIV had been created in Saigon on 6 November 1962 with the mission of field investigations of new methods and new equipment for countering insurgency during actual combat operations. While the soldier-and-scientist teams tested new approaches in many fields (rotary and fixed wing aircraft, communications gear, armored personnel carriers, and the like) ACTIV field evaluators had a major impact on the types of small arms applied to fight the ground war in Vietnam.

Supplies of the test weapons, officially designated Submachine gun XM-177, arrived in November 1966, and were distributed by the end of March 1967. Units receiving test weapons included: 1st, 4th, 9th, and 25th Infantry Divisions; 1st Cavalry Division (Airmobile); 1st Aviation Brigade; 5th Special Forces Group; 11th Armored Cavalry Regiment; 1st Brigade, 101st Airborne Division; 173d Airborne Brigade; and 196th and 199th Light Infantry Brigades. Data collection was carried out from March to May 1967.

Most troops who used the CAR-15 preferred it to the handguns and submachine guns they had previously carried. There was a consensus that the CAR-15 was an ideal weapon for commanders, patrol point men, RTOs (radio telephone operators), FOs (forward observers), dog handlers, and others who needed more compact firepower. Some of those questioned suggested that the CAR-15 should be issued to all officers and NCOs as a "prestige" weapon.

Special units also had a high opinion of the CAR-15. Members of the 5th Special Forces Group were especially enthusiastic: "This light, compact weapon is well-suited for any terrain in which this detachment has operated. It does not rise like the M-16, but does have a definite pull to the right. Accuracy is not decreased by the shortened barrel. It is the general opinion of this detachment that the CAR-15 is far better suited for Special Forces or airborne operations than the M-16 at normal engagement ranges." Scout dog platoons and tracker

The blooding of the M-16

PISTOL PARADE:
Different types of handguns were used during the wars in Indochina. During the final years, the US .45 cal. M-1911A1 (top), the Soviet 7.62 × 25mm Tokarev (PRC Type 51) (center), and the 9 × 18mm Makarov (PRC Type 59) (bottom) were the most popular models.

The blooding of the M-16

ON THE BUTTON: A machine gunner fires his 7.62mm M-60 into a wooded area from which his fellow members of the 25th Infantry Division have taken sniper fire during an operation near Cu Chi in1967. The weapon had been adopted in 1957 as part of the post-1945 modernization of US infantry weapons and used the NATO-standard 7.62mm bullet.

dog teams noted that the CAR-15 was especially good when handling dogs. Only armored vehicle crews were of a mixed mind about the CAR-15. Some wanted a weapon such as the pistol that was always strapped to the crewman, and that did not impede an emergency exit from a vehicle. But nearly all armor personnel favored the CAR-15 to the .45 caliber M-3 submachine gun.

ACTIV staff recommendations were unequivocal. "The CAR-15 SMG (should) be issued as a standard weapon in RVN," and "the M-3 SMG (should) be dropped from the Army inventory." But despite the

early glowing reports from the field, neither the Air Force version of the CAR-15 (the XM-177) nor the Army version with forward assist (the XM-177E1) were destined for success. Numerous minor improvements were made to "tweak" the performance of the XM-177 series weapons. Its barrel was extended a further 38mm to 292mm, and the gun was renamed the XM-177E2.

Still technical problems dogged the weapon. Rates of fire were erratic. Its noise-flash suppressor attachment lost effectiveness due to propellant residue clogging. Ball bullets yawed because of the suppressor, and tracers performed even worse. Fixes were proposed, but money was growing scarce. In the end, a whole host of considerations forced termination of the XM-177 (CAR-15) production in 1970. Special Forces units, SEAL Teams, and other special operations units continued to use and cherish their "Shorties." Long after spare parts began to run low (cannibalization of unserviceable XM-177s was required to keep the weapon operational), these "prestige" weapons could be seen in the midst of some of the toughest fighting.

On the enemy side, the 7.62 × 39mm Soviet designed Avtomat Kalashnikova obrazetsa 1947g and the 7.62 × 39mm Samozaridnya Karabina Simonova obrazetsa 1945g (AK-47 and SKS-45 for short) had become the two basic rifles by the late 1960s. They replaced most older Japanese, French, American, and Soviet pattern rifles for the Viet Cong and the North Vietnamese. The Soviets had emerged from World War II intent upon fielding serviceable lightweight self-loading rifles for their infantry. Long dedicated to massed infantry automatic weapon fire, they had been very impressed by the German development of the Sturmgewehr assault rifles, which used a cartridge of standard 7.92mm caliber, but with a shorter case (33mm vs 57mm long). Short-cased cartridges led to more compact weapons and lighter ammunition loads. During the 1939-45 war the Soviets developed their own short-cased cartridge, the 7.62 × 39mm Model 1943. Soviet military weapon designers competed to create weapons to fire it.

The self-loading 7.62 × 39mm Samozaridnya Karabina Simonova obrazetsa 1945g (SKS-45), designed by Sergei Gavrilovich Simonov, was the first rifle standardized to shoot the new cartridge. Field tested in the final battles of 1945, the SKS was good, but it did not match the evolving tactical doctrine for Soviet motorized infantry. In the jungles and rice paddies of Vietnam it was a useful and effective weapon for guerrilla fighters. Although its smaller size was more suited to the Vietnamese soldier than the older Mausers, Arisakas, and Garands, the SKS still was not as satisfactory for sheer firepower as the extremely rugged AK-47. The latter weapon provided heavy automatic fire, and still was easily managed by Vietnamese troops.

Stock extension —An Air Cav trooper stationed at An Khe demonstrates how to extend the collapsible sliding stock of his 5.56mm XM-177 (CAR-15) submachine gun. This photograph was taken during January 1967 at the time the CAR-15 was being tested by ACTIV personnel.

The blooding of the M-16

SEAL SPECIAL:

A member of the elite US Navy SEAL (Sea-Land-Air) force jumps into the mud in the Mekong Delta carrying a Commando 5.56 machine gun. Based on the CAR-15 carbine/ submachine gun, this XM-177E2 was popularly known as a ''Shortie'' because of its short-length barrel. Despite technical problems that eventually led to its withdrawal, the Shortie was a cherished fighting weapon.

THE AK DYNASTY:
Top: 1964 Soviet RPK light machine gun. Center: mid-1950s Soviet AK-47. Bottom: Polish grenade-launching AK.

MIKHAIL TIMOFEYEVICH KALASHNIKOV, a former NCO armor commander, and father of the AK-47, became interested in firearms theory and design during a long convalescence leave for wounds suffered in World War II. Unfit for immediate return to combat duty, he was assigned to a weapons factory where he pursued design of new small arms. After creating a submachine gun and a carbine that were not accepted for service, he built his AK-47. It became the standard Soviet infantry weapon in

1947. Two basic revisions of the original design were required before the Soviet weapons factories could embark upon large scale production in 1953. It is that version of his assault rifle that was most frequently seen in Vietnam. It was issued in both wood stock and folding stock versions and the Viet Cong had versions of both Soviet and Chinese origin. In 1959, the design bureau led by Kalashnikov and charged with updating and improving his weapon, applied sheet metal stamping techniques to the fabrication of the receiver. The new design was designated the 7.62mm Moderizirovannyiy Avtomat Kalashnikova (AK-M).

As with the 5.56mm M-16 rifle, the 7.62mm AK-47 avtomat was gas operated. The AK-47 design had a conventional piston powered operating rod/bolt carrier mechanism to unlock and lock the bolt. The M-16 rifle used the direct blast of gas (through a gas tube running the length of the barrel) to drive the bolt/bolt carrier assembly to the rear. For hit-and-run warfare, the AK-47 was probably a better design. It required less daily maintenance. From the start, the Kalashnikov had a chrome plated barrel and cartridge chamber. Both the M-16 and the AK-47 could be fired fully automatic or single shot; both used a removable box magazine (30-shot for the AK, 20 and later 30-shot for the M-16); and despite the disparity in caliber they had similar wounding effects out to about 300-400 meters. Beyond that both weapons lost effectiveness as the bullets lost energy and accuracy. At very close ranges (less than 75 meters), the M-16 had the edge in lethality. Both weapons (AK and M-16) were intended to lay down significant quantities of fire, which was employed either to kill the enemy or to suppress his ability to maneuver or return fire.

Unquestionably, Kalashnikov's AK series is among the most successful assault rifle designs, and in the hands of the Viet Cong and NVA it soon made an impression on the US troops who faced it. The first of these weapons was recovered after combat in December 1964 in IV Corps' Chuong Thien Province. The weapons were Chinese Type 56 variants made in 1962. Nearly all NVA and VC units had at least some AK-47s (Type 56s) by the end of 1966. But there was a downside to the arrival of the AK-47 for the VC and the NVA. The weapon

Insignia of US Army Combined Materiel Exploitation Center —Its role was to construct an intelligence picture of enemy weapons and supplies from captured and seized equipment.

was an ammunition eater. Rapid firing assault rifles devoured tons of Soviet and Chinese made cartridges, posing a serious logistic problem. Fire discipline became an important training issue. VC units, such as the 514th Main Force Battalion operating in the Delta's Dinh Tuong Province, established sophisticated ammunition resupply systems. After an engagement, the entire battalion went to a local storage site to obtain more munitions. Usually it took the 514th a single day to be resupplied with ammunition after an attack. This was the result of good preplanning by the rear services unit. Only in the instances of surprise attack by ARVN troops was resupply sometimes delayed. Still, it would only take them two to six days to be resupplied.

It was the operations of these rear supply services that the US and ARVN troops sought to disrupt. In the Delta, shipments came by water and were generally received at a point about 30 minutes' walk from underground storage depots. Shipments arrived irregularly; frequency varying from once every ten days to once every two or three months. Combat units needing weapons or ammunition filed requests with the Province Military Affairs

CAPTURED STOCK: A member of the 7th Bn, Royal Australian Regiment, with a Chinese-made RPD (Type 56) light machine gun captured during heavy fighting at a VC bunker complex. The weapon first made its appearance in Vietnam in 1964.

Committee, which furnished the fighting unit with a delivery order that was presented to the rear services. All movements and supply activities were made at night.

With an adequate supply of ammunition, the Kalashnikov was an effective weapon in ambushes, a favorite Viet Cong tactic. At close ranges (25-100 meters) fire from just a few AK-47s could be devastating for foot soldiers. An essential part of countering ambushes was rapid and massive response. American troops quickly learned to take cover and return automatic fire with their 5.56mm M-16 rifles and their 7.62mm NATO M-60 machine guns.

While a wide variety of machine guns were used on both sides of the conflict, such weapons tended to be too heavy to be practical for long-range patrolling. For this reason the automatic rifle became very popular with all combatants. The heavy and bulky nature of most machine guns encouraged US officials to begin looking at other possible weapons for countering ambushes, the essential aspect of which was surprise. Shotguns, grenade launchers, night vision devices, and snipers were a few effective tools explored for countering VC ambushes.

SHORT-CASED: The Viet Cong were armed with the belt-fed Soviet 7.62mm Degtyarev squad light machine gun (RPD) that used the short-cased 7.62 × 39mm cartridge. First introduced in 1943 the cartridge allowed designers to create more compact weapons requiring lighter ammunition loads.

Stopping power

Shotguns and fléchettes

AS THE FIREPOWER available to the Viet Cong increased, ambushes became a growing and increasingly deadly problem. On the allied side, rifles and machine guns were not sufficient to stop an ambush. Something more effective was necessary. Hand grenades were effective, but the range they could be thrown was very short, particularly when the man throwing it was basically concerned with taking cover. Two weapons were brought to bear on the problem, the 12-gauge (18.5mm) shotgun and the 40mm grenade launchers.

American armed forces have used 12-gauge shotguns since the World War I when they were used in trench fighting. After having served primarily as a prison guard's weapon in World War II and Korea, the 12-gauge was reintroduced both as a patrol weapon and as perimeter protection weapon. In addition to the approximately 50,000 shotguns provided to the South Vietnamese for local defense, the Americans found the shotguns had merit as a front line combat weapon for themselves as well. On patrol the shotgun was an excellent weapon for the point man. As a result, the US Marines began issuing 12-gauge shotguns to their patrols. As a quick-response weapon they were extremely effective.

Units that seriously employed the shotgun always reported higher enemy body counts than other units that did not use such weapons. One of the important trends was towards shorter barrel lengths and larger magazine capacities. The favored model for use in Vietnam was the 8-shot Remington Model 870 Mark I pump-action "riot gun" type, with a 508mm barrel that gave a good spread of double-ought (00 Buck)—nine 9mm lead projectiles. This type of

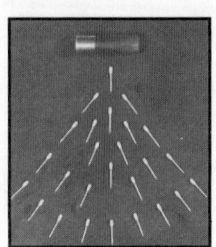

Deadly darts —Fléchette ammunition for the 12-gauge shotgun made an already lethal weapon even more effective. The 25mm steel arrows could wound at ranges out to 50 meters. One 18.5 cal. shotgun cartridge packed 26 fléchettes, each weighing 8 grams.

buckshot load could kill out to 30 meters and inflict serious wounds out to 60 meters. The major drawback to the shotgun was the wide spread of the nine balls. The spread pattern widened rapidly, making it possible to miss a man-sized target. But when a man appeared 5-10 meters in front of its muzzle, the shotgun was a sure killer.

By the mid-1960s, there had been a great deal of experimentation carried out in the United States with "fléchettes," which are best described as 25mm nails with fins. A fléchette had very low mass, but it was fired at high velocity. Although there were serious technical problems with perfecting a single-fléchette rifle cartridge, it occurred to the developers that a group of fléchettes might make a very potent loading for a shotgun shell. Several variants of such shells were issued in Vietnam. These fléchette rounds propelled their light darts (26 in one version) at 570-610 meters per second, and the fléchettes were capable of penetrating flak vests and steel helmets at 400 meters. Unfortunately, the fléchettes did not penetrate the heavy jungle undergrowth. A man behind a meter or two of brush was relatively safe from fléchette shotgun shot.

Both Remington and Winchester-Olin developed fléchette cartridges for 12-gauge shotguns. The Marine Corps designated the Remington round "Cartridge, 12-gauge, Beehive, Remington Model SP-12F-20," and it contained 20 cadmium plated 0.49 gram fléchettes traveling at 594-671 m/s. The Winchester counterpart, the "Cartridge, 18.5mm, fléchette, plastic case" or "Cartridge, 12-gauge shotgun, multiple fléchette, XM258," held twenty 0.47 gram cadmium plated fléchettes traveling at about the same velocity. In both types, the fléchettes were nestled in granulated polyethylene ("grek"), black in the green case Remington cartridges and white in the red Winchester cartridges. Whirlpool, Northrop, AAI, Inc., and Librascope also experimented with fléchette shotgun shells for Vietnam.

Shotgunners generally found that these fléchette loads had their best penetration at ranges beyond 30-35 meters. By that distance they had stopped yawing and had stabilized. At closer ranges, they were yawing and thus produced more serious wounds, but penetration of protective materials was less. Some one-shot kills were reported at ranges of 300 meters, but most effective combat with these loads occurred at 100-110 meters. In Vietnam, where the Marines used the Remington and Winchester rounds interchangeably, the Remington appeared to give greater penetration and tighter patterns at the longer ranges.

The fléchette principle was also applied to artillery rounds. The 105mm howitzer was provided with a "Beehive" shell loaded with some 90,000 fléchettes, which was fitted with an adjustable time fuse. This fuse could be set to burst at any point between the muzzle and the maximum range. When the projectile exploded it released the cloud of fléchettes, which continued along the shell's trajectory. Since the shell was in the air when it burst, and projected the fléchettes downward, there was rarely any foliage between the fléchettes and their targets. American artillerymen soon found another unanticipated use for the Beehive projectiles. With the fuses set for a muzzle burst, the Beehive round could be used to mow down the grass in front of the gun position, thus clearing a field of fire for the local defense machine gunners and denying cover to any marauding Viet Cong. This technique was also found to be useful for flushing out snipers from the undergrowth.

Next to these large caliber artillery fléchette projectiles, all other rounds seemed insignificant. But the infantryman could not carry that type of firepower into combat with him. The next best option was an exploding munition of some sort; hand grenades, rifle grenades, the new 40mm launcher projected grenades, and Claymore mines gave him means of fragging the enemy.

BASE SECURITY:
A 7.62mm sniper rifle with telescopic sight, as used by USAF security police in Vietnam for perimeter security.

The bloop tube

Project NIBLICK and the grenade launcher

SINCE SHOTGUNS were not the complete answer to countering ambushes, an even more destructive weapon was sought. The answer was the M-79, a stubby, short-barreled grenade launcher affectionately called the "bloop tube" or the "blooper" for the sound its muzzle made when fired. Springfield Armory had begun development of this 40 × 46mmSR weapon in the early 1950s, With its large diameter aluminum barrel the M-79 resembled a single-shot break-open sawn-off shotgun. Its basic Vietnam era combat round, the M-406, lobbed a 170-gram high-explosive fragmentation grenade at a velocity of 76 m/s per second to a maximum range of 400 meters.

The M-79 covered the area between the longest range of the hand grenade (30-40 meters) and the middle range of the 60mm mortar (300-400 meters). A basic goal in developing the M-79 grenade launcher was the replacement of traditional rifle launched grenades and 60mm mortars at the squad and platoon level. In the hands of a skilled grenadier, the M-79 was highly accurate to 200 meters, and it turned out to be an excellent weapon for dealing with both jungle ambushes and building-to-building fighting of urban warfare. The M-79 grenade launcher and its ammunition emerged from two separate lines of research: one for smaller size explosive projectiles, and one for a new system of launching such projectiles from a shoulder-fired weapon.

Development of the grenade-type warhead for the weapon that would become the M-79 came out of research conducted by the US Army Ballistic Research Laboratories (BRL) at Aberdeen Proving Ground. By 1951, BRL engineers knew that they

could create such a small but potent explosive package. The question then raised was how to best launch this type of payload. Officers working in the Ordnance small arms research and development shop at the Pentagon, headed by Colonel Rene R. Studler, decided that a dedicated shoulder-fired launcher would be the most appropriate weapon for delivering these grenades.

Jack Bird, deputy to Colonel Studler, took an interest in this project, and created a crude launcher in his off-duty hours. Bird took a short length of golf ball diameter tubing and capped it off at one end. He then drilled some holes in the tube toward the base. After inserting a spring, Bird would drop in a golf ball, push the ball down with a stick (compressing the spring in the process), and then insert a nail to hold the ball in the "cocked position."

When he pulled the "pin," the ball would be launched.

Bird first demonstrated his spring-loaded launcher at the Pentagon in the center courtyard of that uniquely shaped building. Since the golf ball was lobbed much as it would have been if it had been hit with a number nine iron golf club (the Niblick)

Jack Bird suggested that the grenade launcher project be called Project NIBLICK. For the next six years that code name was used for this very secret project.

The Ordnance engineers employed an unusual "high-low pressure system" for launching the new projectile. The method had been developed in Germany during World War II. In the US version, an aluminum cartridge case was used to hold a small propellant charge (330 mg) of M-9 flake-type mortar propellant. The sealed propellant chamber in front of the primer had a number of partially completed, carefully sized holes leading into an expansion chamber area of the case. Upon firing the primer, the propellant created high pressures inside the first chamber that flowed into the larger chamber through the previously prepared holes. Resulting gas pressure in the low pressure chamber produced a low impulse to launch the grenade with both an adequate velocity and an acceptable recoil impulse.

OLD GUARD:

An ARVN soldier keeps watch as his colleagues search a village. His M-1 Garand rifle has a launch adapter fitted with a US fragmentation grenade. It was one of several rifle-based grenade launchers that were replaced by the more accurate, more compact, and easier to use M-79 grenade launcher.

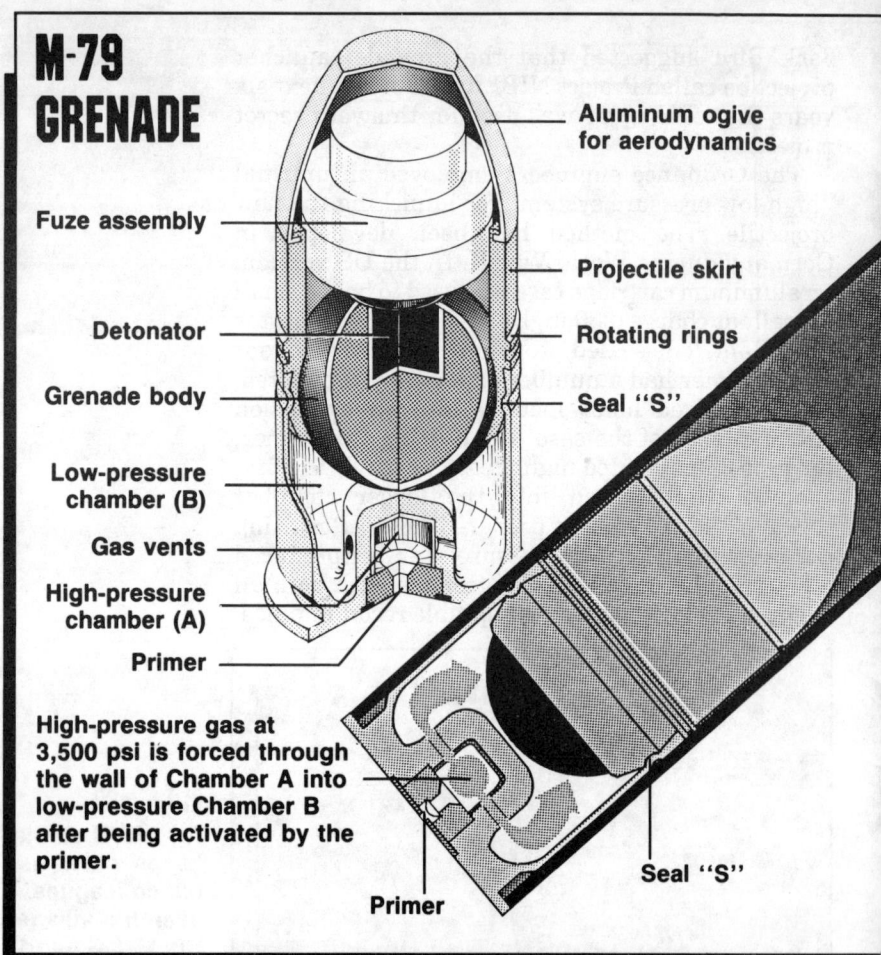

M-79 GRENADE

- Aluminum ogive for aerodynamics
- Fuze assembly
- Detonator
- Grenade body
- Low-pressure chamber (B)
- Gas vents
- High-pressure chamber (A)
- Primer
- Projectile skirt
- Rotating rings
- Seal "S"

High-pressure gas at 3,500 psi is forced through the wall of Chamber A into low-pressure Chamber B after being activated by the primer.

Seal "S"

Primer

By 1953, Cyril Moore, the project leader, and his colleagues at Springfield Armory were launching 40mm grenades from three basic types of launchers; a crude shoulder-fired single-shot launcher, single-shot pistols, and a three-shot shoulder-fired launcher, which had a harmonica-type magazine). When shown the alternative designs, the US Army Infantry Board at first preferred the three-shot launcher, because it produced the greatest firepower. Unfortunately, this repeater was more awkward than the single-shot types and considerably less accurate. Both problems were related to the side moving cartridge holder.

In 1955, just months before Infantry Board testing

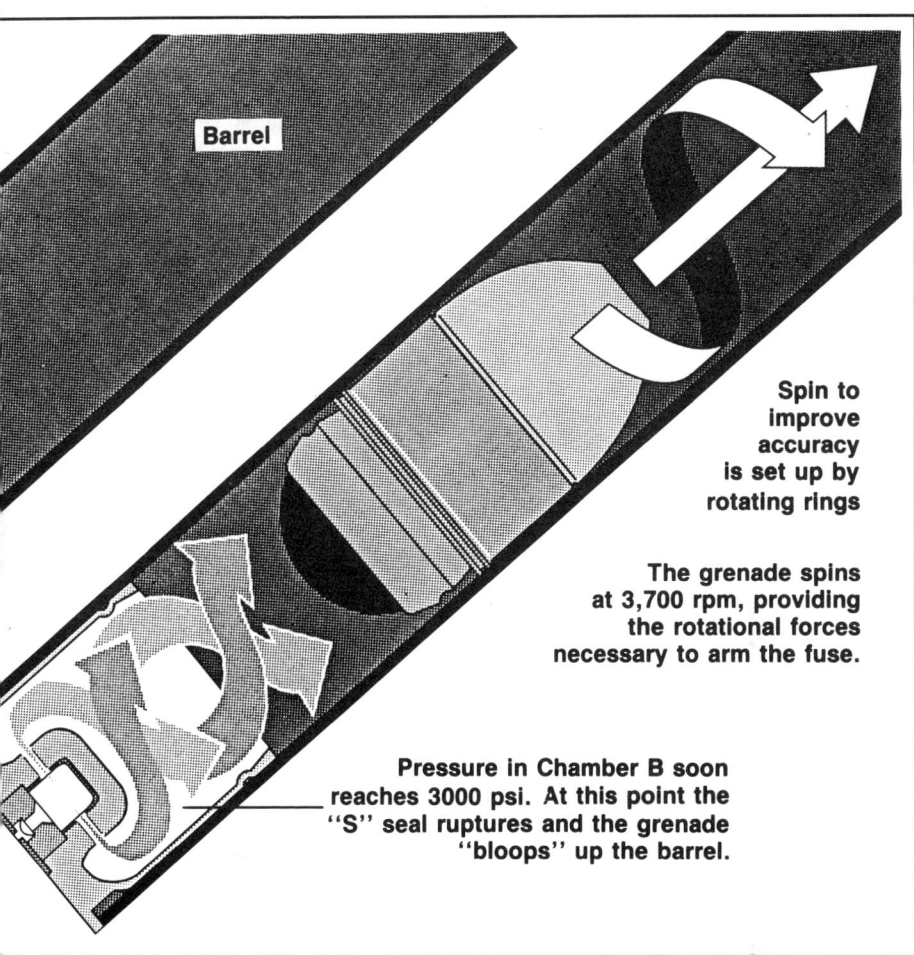

Barrel

Spin to improve accuracy is set up by rotating rings

The grenade spins at 3,700 rpm, providing the rotational forces necessary to arm the fuse.

Pressure in Chamber B soon reaches 3000 psi. At this point the "S" seal ruptures and the grenade "bloops" up the barrel.

of 40mm launchers was scheduled to begin in earnest, Lieutenant Colonel Roy E. Rayle, the Small Arms R&D Chief at Springfield Armory, suggested that a single-shot launcher patterned after the Stevens break-open shotgun might be a better approach than the three-shot launcher. Such a launcher was demonstrated along with the three-shot launcher, and the Infantry Board officials immediately favored the simpler gun. This single-shot launcher—the XM-79—was recommended for standardization by the Board in 1956. It became the M-79 the following year. Six years from initial concept to standardization of a weapon was something of an R&D project record. The first M-79 grenade launchers were delivered to US Army troops in 1961.

M-406 grenades fired from the M-79 contained a charge of high explosive inside a steel casing that produced fragments with a lethal radius of up to 5 meters. (Lethal radius is defined as the area within which 50 percent of exposed troops become casualties.) When the projectile detonates, more than 300 fragments are projected in all directions at 1,524 m/s. In combat, when the grenades detonated (more than 40 percent did not work) the M-406 was a potent addition to the infantryman's repertoire of firepower.

However, the M-79 and its grenades' most significant shortcoming resulted from the fact that the fuse was not armed until the projectile had traveled about 15 meters. At closer ranges, the grenadier had to rely upon his pistol. Thus, shortly after the first M-79 launchers arrived in Vietnam, a cartridge with about 45 fléchettes in a plastic casing was issued on an experimental basis. This round was replaced by another multiple-projectile loading variety, the M-576, which had twenty-seven 00 Buckshot. In this M-576 buckshot round, the pellets were carried down the barrel in a 40mm plastic sabot, the design of which caused it to slow down in flight so the pellets

HIGH-LOW COMPARISON: A 40 × 46mm low-velocity shoulder-fired grenade cartridge (top) and a 40 × 53mm high velocity cartridge created for aircraft and vehicle-mounted multi-shot weapons (bottom). The high-velocity cartridge required a smaller high-low pressure chamber and needed more propellant.

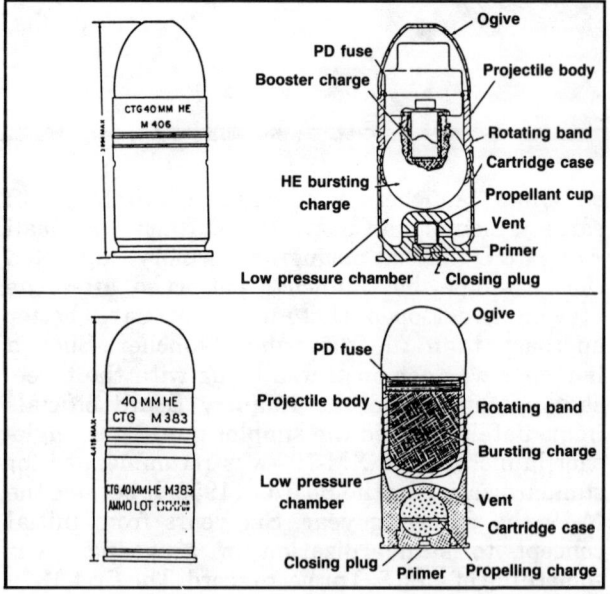

could travel forward on their own. Both of these rounds were highly deadly at short range.

Before production ended in 1971, in favor of the M-203 grenade launcher, about 350,000 M-79s were made for the government by a group of contractors—Springfield Armory (pilot line production), Kanarr Corporation, Action Manufacturing Corporation, TRW Inc., Varo Inc., and Exotic Metals Corporation.

US Army personnel had one major complaint about the M-79. Since it was a dedicated weapon, there was at least one less rifleman in the squad. It simply was not practical for the grenadier—the name assigned to the individual carrying the grenade launcher—to carry both the M-79 and a rifle. It was just a short intellectual leap from the realization of this problem to the idea of building a launcher that could be attached to a rifle. Prototypes of such weapons had been tested in the latter years of the NIBLICK project and in the Special Purpose Individual Weapon (SPIW) project (1961-66). The next step was the attachment of such a device to the AR-15 rifle.

Robert E. Roy, a Colt engineer who earlier worked on Project NIBLICK, created a simple under-the-barrel launcher for the AR-15 in 1964 to test out the idea. Once the Colt people were certain that the concept would work, they set up a more formal project to develop a service-type launcher. This work, directed by Carl Lewis and Rob Roy, led to the Colt CGL-4 grenade launcher (XM-148 in Army terminology). The combat suitability of the XM-148 was yet another of the projects investigated by the Army Concept Team in Vietnam.

In November 1966, the Army Staff at the Pentagon asked ACTIV personnel to study the 40mm XM-148 grenade launcher. Meanwhile, this launcher was placed in the hands of 1,734 US troops in Vietnam by January 1967. From 23 January to 4 February, Rob Roy and Kanemitsu Ito of Colt, accompanied by three men from the US Army Weapons Command, instructed nearly 400 individuals in the use of the XM-148 launcher. Within a few months each brigade-size unit (about 4,000 men) had 254 XM-148 grenade launchers.

Meanwhile, ACTIV staffers tested the effectiveness of the XM-148 and its suitability as a combat weapon. Their sample of users and small unit

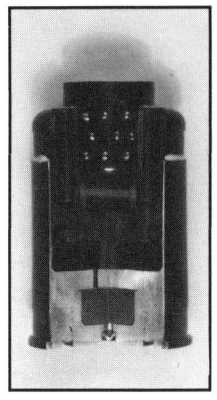

Inside view—This cut-away of the 40 × 46mmSR M-79 XM-576E1 multiple projectile buckshot cartridge, shows the air pockets in the face of the plastic sabot and the positioning of the buckshot.

leaders included men from four different divisions and seven separate brigades and covered the entire spectrum of Vietnamese terrain and climate. Some unusual findings resulted from analysis of their returned questionnaires. The most significant was that squad and platoon leaders were concerned that grenadiers often chose the comforting sound of the rifle being fired rather than shooting the launcher portion of their XM-16E1/XM-148 weapon combination, thereby losing the benefit of the explosive effect of the 40mm grenades. Clearly, training, fire discipline, and doctrinal decisions were needed to more fully integrate the rifle/grenade launcher weapon system into the squad's combat firepower.

Although the performance of the XM-148 was satisfactory in terms of range and signature (noise and muzzle flash) when compared to the M-79, there were some early and persistent complaints about its operational reliability. Chief concerns involved difficulty in cocking the launcher, awkwardness of the battle sight, and worries about the basic safety of the XM-148. There was also some concern expressed about the robustness of the XM-148's components. Still, in open country, a majority of grenadiers preferred the XM-148 to the M-79. In thick vegetation opinion was divided over the two weapons. Fire leaders, platoon sergeants and most officers preferred the M-79 by a 2 to 1 margin.

After evaluating all of their data, the ACTIV team concluded, in a May 1967 report, that "the XM-148 in its present configuration is unsatisfactory for further operational use in Vietnam." They recommended that all of these launchers be withdrawn from combat units, and be replaced with M-79 grenade launchers. While the XM-148 failed, the concept of a rifle-mounted 40mm grenade launcher had been proven to be a valuable one. The ACTIV investigators went on to recommend an expedited R&D project to develop a better weapon of the XM-148 type.

Despite the fact that all XM-148s were withdrawn from allied units, the author had the opportunity in 1972 to examine one at the ARVN 30th Base Arsenal in Saigon. It had been much modified into a shoulder-fired launcher (without rifle) by the Viet Cong. Worn and battered, it obviously had seen considerable use by some VC who likely was happy

Mortar variant —This Springfield Armory 40 × 46mm breech-loading mini-mortar, known as a "ground support launcher" was one of several experimental variants of the basic grenade launcher. Although thought interesting, it offered no advantages over the shoulder-fired launchers and was never put into production.

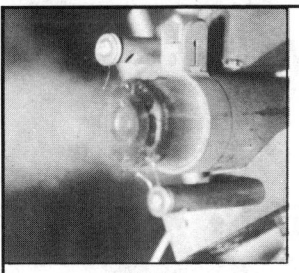

Muzzle

12 inches from muzzle

4 feet from muzzle

5 feet from muzzle

to have the firepower it offered him and his comrades.

Back in the United States, the US Army Materiel Command created, as a result of the ACTIV recommendations, the GLAD (Grenade Launcher Attachment Development) program to develop a better M-16-mounted grenade launcher. Contracts were let, in the fall of 1967, with three companies (AAI, Inc., Aeronutronic Division of Philco-Ford, and Aero-Jet General Corporation), and work was soon underway on new rifle mounted grenade launchers under the supervision of the Springfield Armory.

The successful GLAD candidate was the M-203 Grenade Launcher created by AAI, Inc. This 40mm weapon consisted of a short aluminum tube clamped underneath the M-16 rifle barrel. It had a forward moving slide-operated breech. It allowed a grenadier to carry a standard rifle for self-defense, and have a loaded grenade launcher as well. Because the M-203 had a shorter barrel than the M-79 launcher, the maximum range of the grenade was reduced to 325 meters and its accurate effective range to 125 meters. Under combat conditions, this was a small sacrifice for a considerable tactical gain.

In April 1969, 500 XM-203 grenade launchers

The blooper tube

SIMPLE BUT UNSAFE: A rifleman with the 2d Bn, 502d Infantry, 101st Airborne Bde, recons by fire with his M-16A1 rifle mounted with an 40mm XM-148 grenade launcher in September 1967. A few weeks later the weapon was withdrawn from service and troops had to wait two years before its replacement, the M-203 grenade launcher, was available. Right: A disassembled view of the XM-148 grenade launcher and the XM-16E1 rifle illustrates how the two were attached. Although plagued with safety complaints, nearly everyone applauded the XM-148s basic simplicity.

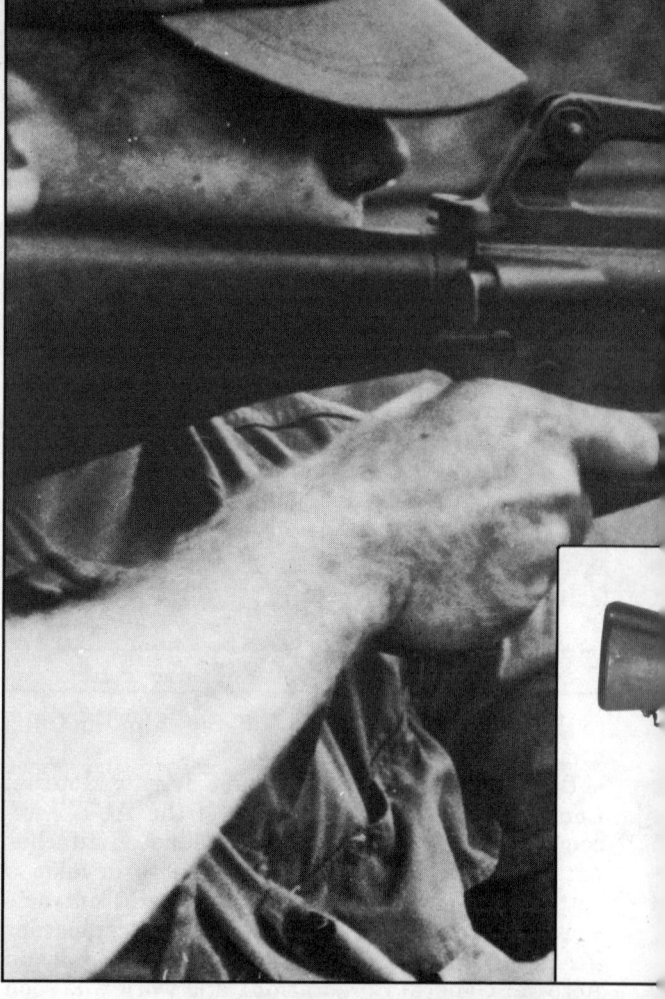

were sent to Vietnam for testing. They were distributed to the 1st, 4th, and 25th Infantry Divisions, the 101st Airborne Division (Airmobile), and the 11th Cavalry Regiment during a three-month-long evaluation. After weapons instruction on operation and maintenance by a seven-man New Equipment Training Team (NETT), the XM-203s were employed in actual operational combat missions between 7 April and 18 June in I, II, and III Corps.

During these tests most rounds were fired for "reconnaissance by fire" and shots against exposed enemy personnel. According to an ACTIV report: "It was generally believed that the enemy was more likely to expose himself when initially engaged with

40mm high-explosive (HE) rounds rather than rifle fire. Personnel armed with the XM-203 normally fired 40mm HE rounds at a suspected target and then covered the area with their M-16 rifle while waiting for the enemy to break and run. This technique was effective, resulting in several confirmed kills during the evaluation period." In one case, a group of VC were surprised on a trail and one shot killed three men. Bunkers were another common target. Enemy soldiers were usually engaged at less than 50 meters by the point man in a patrol. And in one instance, a point man killed a VC at less than 10 meters with a round of 40mm XM-576E1 buckshot.

Reported varieties of combat loads of 5.56mm rifle

ammunition and 40mm grenade cartridges included:

—Thirteen magazines of 5.56mm (20-shot capacity) and 25 rounds of 40mm HE.

—Eight magazines of 5.56mm, 40 rounds of 40mm HE, and 6 rounds of 40mm buckshot.

—Ten magazines of 5.56mm, 30 rounds of 40mm HE, and 10 rounds of 40mm buckshot.

A few soldiers carried 40mm pyrotechnic or CS gas cartridges. This was generally influenced by the availability of these experimental rounds. Some grenadiers carried one pyrotechnic round, others carried as many as five.

At the start of ACTIV's study of the XM-203, the army recommended that the M-79 be retained in many rifle squads. However, most units involved exchanged their M-79s for XM-203s. In one instance, a unit retained the M-79 at first, but once men became familiar with the M-203 they turned in their old "bloop tubes." After three months of field tests, the ACTIV team enthusiastically endorsed the XM-203 and recommended that, with some minor modifications, the launcher should replace all of the M-79s in Vietnam. It took some time to get the needed M-203 grenade launchers built. The AAI cororation was not equipped to mass produce small arms. After the initial 600 M-203s had been manuactured by AAI, Inc., production of this grenade launcher was shifted to Colt in 1971. Only a small number of M-203s were actually available for

delivery to Vietnam in the last years of the war and most went to US personnel. The ARVN, which had received a total of 70,601 M-79 grenade launchers by 1975, received only 249 XM-148s and 76 M-203s.

In addition to the shoulder-fired 40 × 46mmSR grenade launchers there were a series of limited production and experimental multiple-shot grenade launchers used in Vietnam. These included the low-velocity 40 × 46mmSR XM-174 automatic Army launcher and the MK 10 MOD 0 hand-cranked Navy launcher, and the high-velocity 40 × 53mmSR Army XM-175, XM-182, Navy M-K 19 MOD 0 and MK 20 MOD 0, and Colt CROW (Counter Recoil Operated Weapon) launchers. High-velocity ammunition, in addition to having a longer cartridge case and heavier projectiles, had a different type of "high-low" launching system that produced higher velocities (244 m/s versus 76 m/s) and the greater recoil energies needed to operate automatic launchers. This ammunition was originally developed for the M-75 and M-129 externally powered helicopter-mounted grenade launchers. The desire for increased vehicle and boat-mounted firepower led to experiments with self-actuated, electrically powered and hand-cranked 40mm launchers. However, the numbers produced and used in Vietnam for any one of these variants numbered in the low hundreds as opposed to the tens of thousands for the M-79 and M-203 shoulder-ired models.

LIMITED EXPERIMENT 2:

The 40 × 53mm high-velocity MK 19 MOD 0 grenade launching machine gun developed by the US Navy was introduced later in the war on an experimental basis. While far from perfect, it did provide a major new source of significant firepower. Here sailors from River Division 152 man a MK 19 mounted atop an M-113 APC during combat in Tay Ninh Province in July 1969.

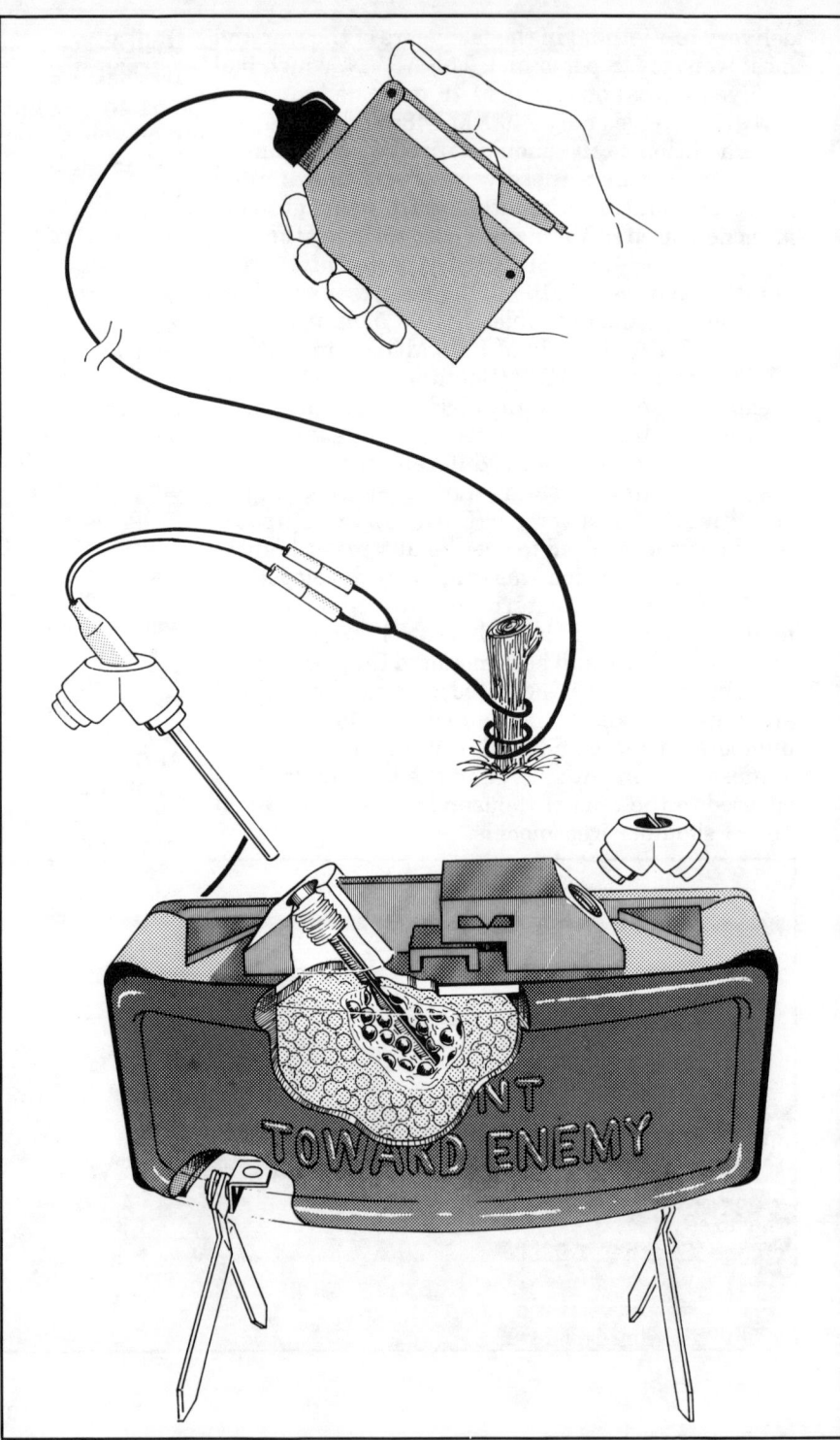

Ambush specials

8

Anti-personnel mines

AS THE WAR developed both US and ARVN forces tried to switch from being the ambushed to becoming the ambushers. When Viet Cong units became too set in their routines, the American and South Vietnamese troops were able to set effective traps for them. It was important for allied forces to keep constant pressure on the Viet Cong. By constantly disrupting his supply and personnel infiltration routes, they were able to strangle the VC's much needed support. One of the best tactical examples of constant pressure were the ambushes executed by the Riverine Brigade in Kien Hoa Province.

At first the Riverine Brigade had lived aboard ship, sallying forth for reconnaissance-in-force missions. In the fall of 1968, the 3d Battalion, 47th Infantry Regiment, 9th Infantry Division broke from this pattern and created a base camp in a coconut grove that spanned several of the main highways and canals in the province. This move led to improved intelligence, and allowed the men of the 3d Battalion to set up and spring effective ambushes. These ambushes became very effective through the use of snipers, radar, and sensor networks.

The 3d of the 47th derived much of its ambush firepower from M-79 grenade launchers and Claymore mines. "When the Viet Cong entered the killing area," a report later stated, "the ambush was initiated by the detonation of the Claymore belts and the area was sealed with M-79 fire augmented by direct fire weapons. Artillery fires were adjusted into the area of contact and along likely avenues of escape." As their combat experience demonstrated, the Claymore mine was one of the most lethal weapons for its size ever produced.

The Claymore (or Mine, Antipersonnel, M-18A1)

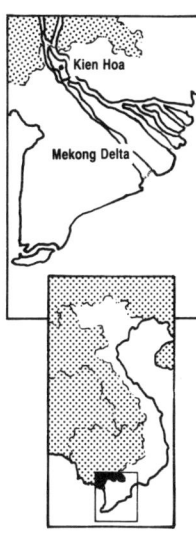

Kien Hoa

Mekong Delta

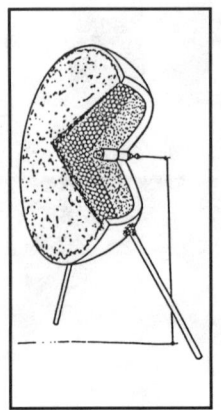

Deadly dish—The Viet Cong fixed, directional fragmentation DH-5 mine. Packed with hundreds of steel pellets and 5 pounds of explosives these electrically command-detonated "Claymore" type anti-personnel mines were extremely devastating weapons when used in ambushes.

was yet another military idea evolved from World War II German technology. The original version consisted of a slab of explosive with a slightly hollow front face. That concave surface was lined with a thick steel plate. It was intended as an antitank weapon. When the explosive was detonated it threw the plate forward in one piece with sufficient velocity and energy to break through tank armor at 50 meters. Fortunately for the World War II Allies, the Germans never fully developed this idea. During the Korean War, as a response to North Korean and Chinese mass-attacks, American ordnance specialists adapted this concept to propelling small pieces of steel. But this experimental antipersonnel device was not ready for service before the Korean War ended.

This promising line of R&D was continued, and resulted in the M-18 series of command-detonated Claymore mines. The version used in Vietnam (M-18A1) had a curved olive-drab molded fiberglass-filled polystyrene case—216mm long, 83mm high, and 35mm deep—filled with 0.68 kg of C4 plastic explosive, in the face of which were buried 700 steel spheres. The shape of the casing and the facing of the explosive was so designed that when the mine was detonated, with the M-57 firing device, the resulting blast projected the spheres in a 60-degree fan-shaped arc, with a velocity that was lethal to a range of 50 meters.

In fixed defensive positions Claymore mines were used in depth, with overlapping kill zones. They were also very effective in opening an ambush because of the extensive, instantaneous lethal zone generated, and because they did not reveal the location of the ambush patrol. The ingenuity and speed with which Claymores were positioned became a matter of professional pride with US infantrymen in Vietnam. The Claymore's effectiveness has insured it a lasting place in the US Army arsenal.

During the period July 1968 to March 1969, the 9th Infantry Division conducted 16,848 ambushes, the equivalent of more than 60 ambushes every night. The success rate (enemy killed, and equipment captured) was excellent. Much of the credit for the success of these ambushes went to the infantryman's personal firepower. Two important elements that enhanced the effect of the Claymores

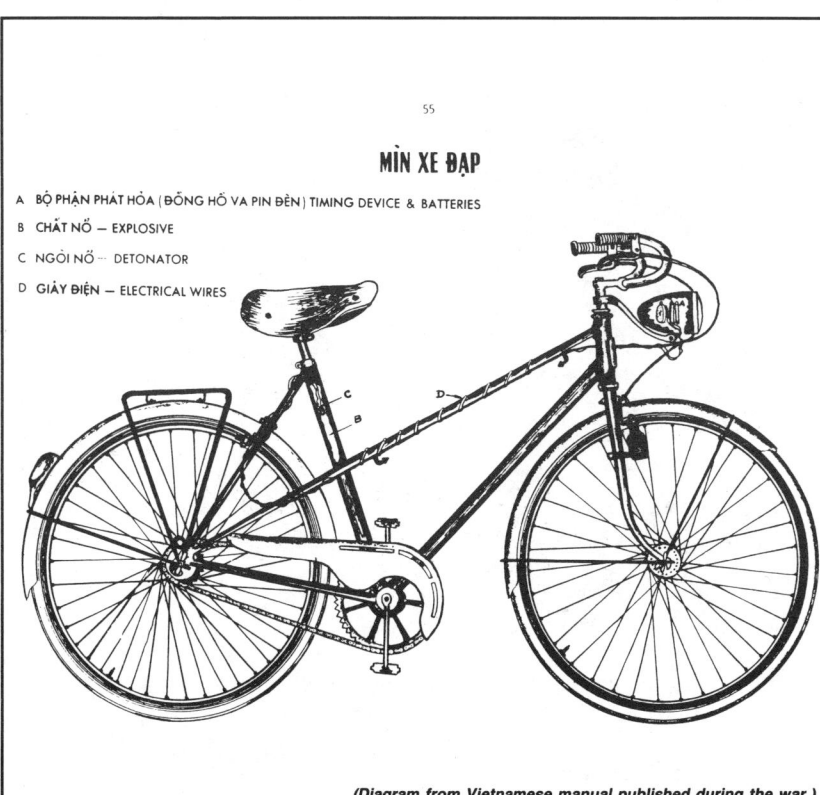

55

MÌN XE ĐẠP

A BỘ PHẬN PHÁT HỎA (ĐỒNG HỒ VA PIN ĐÈN) TIMING DEVICE & BATTERIES
B CHẤT NỔ — EXPLOSIVE
C NGÒI NỔ — DETONATOR
D GIÂY ĐIỆN — ELECTRICAL WIRES

(Diagram from Vietnamese manual published during the war.)

and the M-79s were new night vision devices and highly trained snipers. "Using intelligence, stealth, cunning, and aggressive tactics the 3d Battalion 47th Infantry and other battalions in the Division were able to take the night away from the Viet Cong by interdicting his route of communications thus upsetting his time schedule, his flow of supplies, and his personnel," an official report later stated.

On the enemy side, the Viet Cong mastered an extreme variety of improvised explosive devices (IED) built from unexploded artillery shells and aerial bombs. In addition to such man-tripped and command-detonated booby traps, the VC used large numbers of saucer shaped DH-10 mines, a larger version of the Claymore. These 300mm diameter directional mines each weighed 9 kg and had 4.5 kg of cast TNT to propel 420-450 cylindrical pellets, and proved to be extremely effective killers of men and helicopters.

THE BICYCLE BOMB: Viet Cong sappers created booby traps out of ordinary objects. The bicycle mine could be parked anywhere without drawing suspicion. Explosives were packed into the seat tube and were detonated by a delayed action fuse and watch concealed inside the front lamp.

111

Night eyes

Light-intensifying night sights

ONE OF THE COMMONEST expressions of the war was that "the night belongs to Charlie." US, ARVN, and allied forces at first operated only during daylight, while the VC moved and fought under the cover of darkness. Even when the battlefield was illuminated by flares and pyrotechnic devices it was difficult to maneuver. As a result, night operations were disliked by commanders and troops alike, and were rarely as successful as they should have been.

This created pressure and interest at all levels in the perfection of light-intensifying night sight devices that would permit soldiers to see in the dark. During the latter stages of World War II, the US Army had developed infrared night sights for light weapons. These devices, which used infrared spotlights to illuminate the night, never gained widespread acceptance by US troops. One reason was detectability. Infrared spotlights could be seen by an enemy equipped with an optical viewer sensitive to the infrared portion of the spectrum.

Brigadier General John K. Boles, Jr., Director of the Department of Defense Joint Research and Test Activity (JRATA) in Vietnam was a strong advocate of infrared (IR) night vision equipment. General Boles encouraged tests of such hardware by US troops in Vietnam. JRATA had the South Vietnamese troops test the Polan P-155 night vision weapon sight. Special mounts were prepared by the US Army Limited War Laboratory for the M-1 rifle, M-1 carbine, M-16 rifle, M-1919A4 light machine gun, and M-79 grenade launcher. The goal of this project was to determine if this type of equipment should be issued to ARVN troops.

Between 31 March and 14 July 1965 fifty P-155 IR sights were distributed to ARVN Special

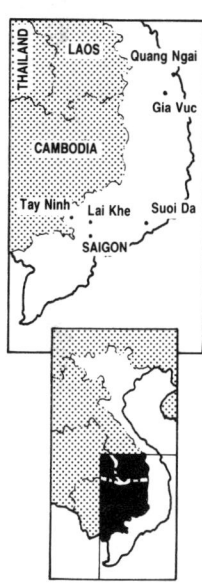

Night eyes

NIGHT WATCH:
A soldier in Vietnam sights through an AN/PVS-2 Starlight imaging intensifying scope mounted on his M-16 rifle. This sight could be hand held or could be mounted, as it is here, on a weapon.

Forces—Infantry, Ranger, Airborne battalions, and to Vietnamese Navy River Assault Groups for the field phase of the project. The equipment—a light source, telescopic sight, and power source—tested in I, II, III, and IV Corps tactical zones, weighed 14 kg. It was designed to operate for up to five hours of continuous use on one charging of the batteries, and it was expected to permit observation of targets out to 300 meters. In actual practice, these Polan night vision weapon sights were useful out to about 175 meters with the average usage range being 100 meters. As with most ACTIV projects, the tests of these sights were carried out under actual combat conditions.

The first test usage of infrared sights took place at the Suoi Da Special Forces Camp in Tay Ninh Province on the night of 1 April 1965. This camp was manned by four Cambodian and two Vietnamese Civilian Irregular Defense Group (CIDG) companies. In this test the sights were mounted on a .30 caliber (7.62 × 63mm) M-1919A4 light machine gun and on a .30 caliber (7.62 × 25mm) M-1 carbine. It became immediately apparent that the bunker-mounted machine gun could not be used because the firing aperture was too small to permit the light source of the sight to shine out. The camp commander refused to relocate the machine gun. The carbine-mounted sight was deployed, instead, on the top of another

INSIDE THE STARLIGHT SCOPE:
A diagram of the internal intensifier tube, the heart of the AN/PVS-2 Starlight imaging intensifying scope. The intensifier could amplify contrast between objects up to 60,000 times so that a scene in starlight, which appeared almost black to the naked eye, could be viewed as if it were in daylight.

bunker that had sandbag walls. The weapon was nested in sandbags to relieve the operator of the combined weight of the weapon, telescope, and light source. The infrared beam repeatedly reflected back from the concertina and barbed wire that surrounded the bunker. In addition, the sight did not provide vision to the outer perimeter barbed wire some 175 meters away.

Three weeks later, on 24 April, a Montagnard CIDG platoon-size patrol departed the Gia Vuc Special Forces Camp in northern Quang Ngai Province to set up an ambush at a trail junction along the Song Re River. The patrol had two IR sights; one on an M-1 carbine and one on a M-16 rifle. At about 0500 hours on 25 April, the point man reported that he saw men moving in the riverbed. The infrared sight operator reported ten Viet Cong crossing the river away from the patrol at 75 meters' distance. He opened fire as did another member of the patrol. The infrared sight operator reported that three Viet Cong had been hit. One had dropped behind some large rocks; another was floating face down in the water; the third was sprawled out on top of a rock in the riverbed. The remaining VC escaped.

In other operations with the IR night sights troops spotted VC personnel but the ARVN patrol held their fire to avoid giving their position away.

Attempts to use night scopes from aircraft and riverine patrol craft were unsuccessful. The

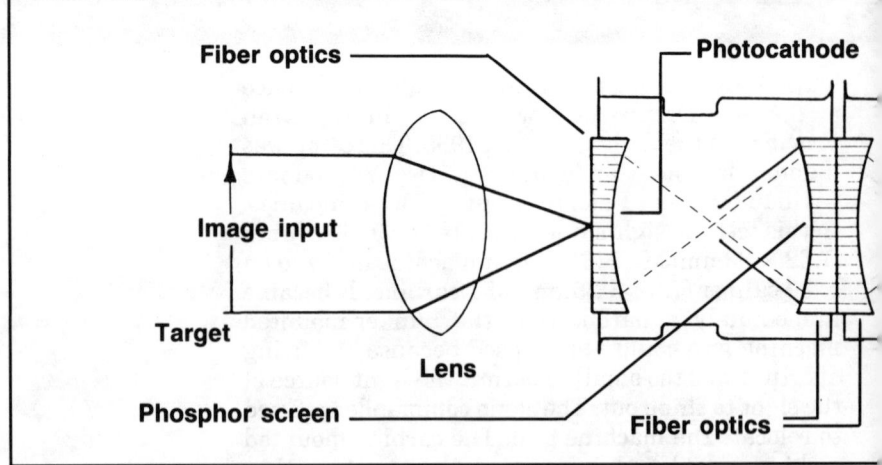

Fiber optics — Photocathode

Image input

Target

Lens

Phosphor screen — Fiber optics

telescopic portion of the night sight had a narrow field of view and images seen through it were easily blurred by the motion of an aircraft or a boat. In 79 nights of usage the IR weapons sights were credited with three VC KIA confirmed, three VC KIA unconfirmed, one VC WIA unconfirmed, and one VC captured.

One major drawback to the entire evaluation process was the fear expressed by ARVN and US commanders that such equipment might fall into enemy hands. The commander of the ARVN 44th Infantry Regiment insisted that a company of his men accompany each IR sight to protect it. The biggest technical complaint—by Americans and Vietnamese—was the excessive weight and the attendant awkwardness associated with the IR night vision sights. As a result of this evaluation, the ACTIV staff concluded that while the Polan P-155 IR night weapon sight met its design characteristics except for range, it was "undesirable to issue infrared weapon sights to the RVNAF units because:

—The sight was too heavy for the average Vietnamese soldier.

—Most RVNAF units did not have available . . . electrical facilities . . . to charge nickel-cadmium batteries. None had such facilities when on operations away from base stations.

—Weapon sights were not used enough to justify their issue to RVNAF units.

General Boles was disappointed with the reaction

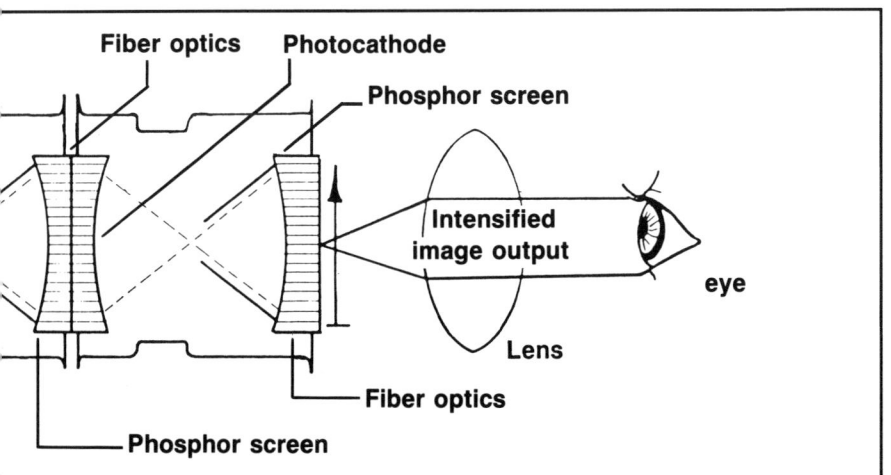

117

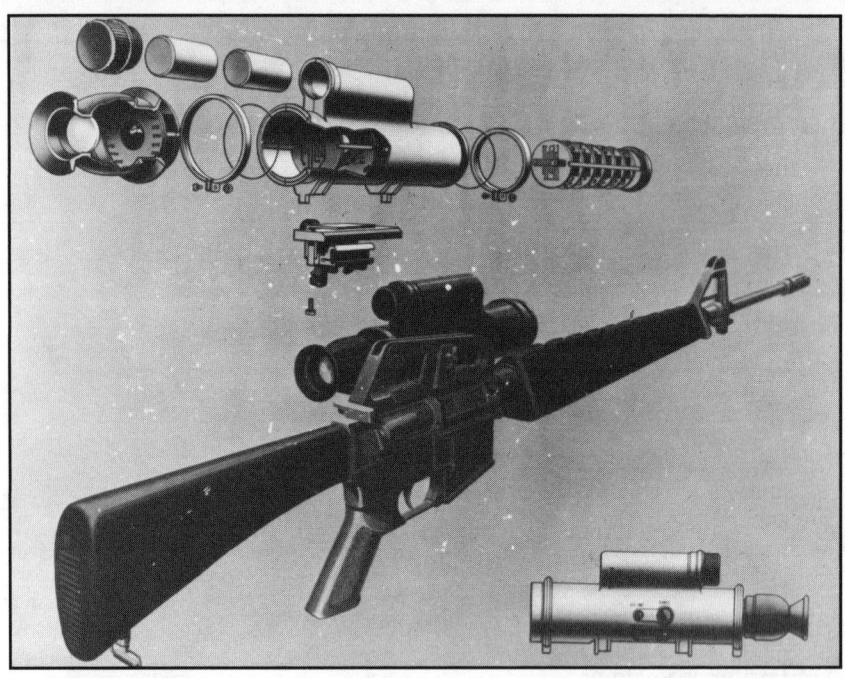

of the ARVN troops. He believed that the "advantages of the system outweigh the disadvantages and the sight gives an advantage to the using units in certain situations." Where flares and other conventional light-making devices often benefited the enemy as much as the friendly troops, "infrared night vision devices, on the other hand, are of no benefit to the enemy and certainly increase the capabilities of the friendly troops." As for sights falling into the hands of the enemy, after the batteries discharged, the VC would have found it virtually impossible to recharge them.

While the General was disappointed by the ARVN reaction to this specific sight, it was clear that night vision equipment of an advanced form would be very valuable to American and allied troops. He forecast: "The newer models of the light intensification sights have about one-third or one-fourth the bulk of the infrared sight, have about one-half the overall weight of the night weapon sight system and because of their not having a requirement for a heavy battery which requires recharging, will not present the difficulties associated with the recharging of batteries." Since the Starlight scopes were more portable, General Boles concluded: "It may be that the light intensification devices will have advantages which outweigh the disadvantages attributed to the infrared night vision sight by the RVNAF."

Although "active" night vision devices were scrapped for infantry battlefield use, R&D continued with "passive" night vision devices. With the post-1945 advances in electronic technology, a technique was developed to use an optical lens to detect small amounts of light, and convert this light into electronic signals. The signals were amplified electronically, and then converted back into a visual picture which could be viewed in an optical eyepiece. Such devices did not work in total darkness (some contrast between objects was required so that there was something to be amplified), but even limited contrast could be magnified up to 60,000 times. Thus a scene in starlight, which appeared black to the unaided eye, could be viewed as if it were daylight through the image intensifier. The other great advantage of this type of sight lay in the absence of any visible signal. It could not be detected by the enemy. The first indication he had of the presence of such equipment was when the bullets begin to strike.

How it looked —An operator's eye view of a target through a Starlight scope. Image intensifying produced just discernible silhouettes rather than sharp outlines.

General Boles and his colleagues knew these new sights could make a major difference in night combat. In October 1965, four months following the completion of ACTIV tests on the IR sight, the Military Assistance Command Vietnam (MACV) requested test samples of light intensification devices—Small Starlight Scope (SSS); Crew-Served Weapon Night Vision Sight (CSWS); Medium Range Night Observation Device (NOD); and Helmet Mounted Infrared Binoculars (IRB)—for possible use by American and ARVN troops. An ACTIV evaluation team arrived in Vietnam on 25 February 1966 to begin tests with the devices in a variety of combat operations.

On one of these, an ambush patrol of the 2d Brigade, 28th Infantry, 1st Infantry Division, located at Lai Khe, used the Small Starlight Scope to detect a company-size Viet Cong force moving toward their position. As the patrol prepared to open fire, its leader, using his Starlight device, discovered a second company-size VC unit moving in just

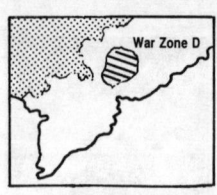

Location of War Zone D where troops of the 173d Airborne Brigade used Starlight scopes to spring a defensive trap.

behind the first group. The patrol leader allowed the first section to pass so his men could ambush the second one. When the first group of VC returned to the sound of the fight, they started shooting at the other VC unit. Meanwhile, the American patrol withdrew and called in artillery fire. Although the US patrol leader was killed during the action, the surviving platoon sergeant credited the Starlight Scope with saving their lives. Without it they would not have seen the second VC company, and would have jeopardized their own survival. The platoon sergeant reported that the Starlight Scope was one of the most useful pieces of equipment he had ever used in battle.

In another action, a patrol of the 2d Battalion, 502d Infantry, 101st Airborne Division operating southwest of Tuy Hoa in Phu Yen Province in II Corps was returning to its lines. The patrol leader had been instructed to return along a specific rice paddy dike that led to the platoon's perimeter. At night all dikes looked alike, and there were dozens of dikes. The patrol leader had arranged to have a guide to be stationed at the end of the correct dike, and with his Small Starlight Scope he was able to detect the guide at a distance of 300 meters, and then work their way safely back to their own lines. Without the Starlight Scope they would have had to guess which dike was the correct one, in the process they might have been mistaken for a VC force moving about in the night.

In defensive situations, the light-intensifying night vision devices were even more effectively used. Of 127 men interviewed, 118 reported that they had used their night vision devices to spot enemy forces during defensive operations. The Small Starlight Scope was used at listening posts, as was the Crew-Served Weapon Night Vision Sight (CSWS) mounted on .50 caliber machine guns.

A typical defensive employment of the Small Starlight Scope occurred on 15 March 1966 when an element of the 173d Airborne Brigade in VC War Zone D, the area due north of Saigon in III Corps Tactical Zone, was on guard against enemy attack. At 0100 hours, under light conditions equal to a half moon, an observation post night vision device operator detected and identified six enemy troops moving along an adjacent ridge line. He called

artillery fire onto this target. At the completion of the fire mission, the operator, looking through his Starlight scope, was able to count the dead bodies.

During the same month, men of the 1st Battalion, 5th Cavalry, 1st Cavalry Division were conducting a mission to secure Route 19 at the An Khe Pass. For six consecutive nights VC forces tried to infiltrate the battalion's command post area. Each time the VC were detected under lighting conditions varying from a new moon to a quarter moon. Significantly, they were noticed before they got close enough to throw hand grenades. Once the enemy had been spotted, the observation post called for illumination flares and mortar fire. This firepower, together with tracer fire from machine guns, was sufficient to beat back the attacks. During this period three VC were confirmed KIA, four were captured, and there was evidence of other casualties.

The 3d Brigade, 1st Infantry Division used the CSWS in conjunction with the AN/PPS-4 ground

PERIMETER WATCH: A member of the 2d Bde, 9th Infantry uses an AN/PVS-2 Starlight scope to scan the perimeter of the base at Dong Tam. The smallest of the scopes, it had a range of up to 300 meters.

Night eyes

FAR-SIGHTED: A .50 cal. (12.7 × 99mm) M-2 heavy barrel machine gun crew demonstrates the Crew Served Weapon Night Vision Sight that allowed them to see in the dark out to a range of 1,800 meters. This sight/gun combination gave perimeter defense teams a real operational edge over the Viet Cong.

surveillance radar to spot enemy movements around their Base Camp at Lai Khe. The CSWS and radar unit watched over the camp area from atop a 23-meter tower. While the Crew Served Weapon Sight allowed surveillance out to 1,800 meters, the radar could monitor movements out to 6,000 meters (6 kilometers). Together, the ACTIV personnel argued, these two systems helped to deprive Charlie of his best ally—the night.

Because the Small Starlight Scope had performed well tactically and technologically, the ACTIV staff urged the Pentagon to provide sufficient Starlight Scopes to provide one per rifle squad, one per M-60 machine gun, and one per infantry platoon headquarters, plus a ten percent reserve for

replacements. In time this rifle-mounted Small Starlight Scope was designated the AN/PVS-2 Starlight Scope and proved extremely popular with infantrymen in the field.

By contrast the ACTIV team and the US Army Combat Developments Command at Fort Belvoir, Virginia, remained uncertain about the value of the Crew Served Weapons Sight or the still larger Night Vision Device. More data was required before they could make firm recommendations about their suitability for combat. They needed to determine if they were rugged enough and sufficiently environment-proof for use in Vietnam. Ultimately these sights were fielded with very positive effects.

Reach out and touch someone

10

Sniper rifles

STARLIGHT NIGHT VISION SCOPES were particularly effective when used as part of the US Army's sniper program. While the US military had previously used snipers in combat, the systematic training and employment in Vietnam of an aggressive, offensive sniper team was something new. Early in the active use of American troops in Vietnam, some US Army and US Marine Corps commanders saw the importance of having snipers to counter the active sniper threat posed by the enemy, and these same "shooters" could harass the enemy's sense of well-being. While the Marine Corps had revived sniper/scout training in 1960, the Army had let its preparation of such personnel fade away about that same time. It took the Vietnam conflict to bring about the development of new sniper weapons and the training of a new generation of long-distance killers.

The Marine Corps took the first steps toward fielding fully qualified snipers in mid-1965. The Army followed in the spring of 1966. Captain E. J. Land, USMC, was one of the spark plugs of the sniper revival in the US armed forces. In 1960, Land had noted for his superiors that "there is an extremely accurate, helicopter-transportable, self-supporting weapon available to the Marine Infantry Commander. This weapon, which is easily adapted to either the attack or defense, is the M-1C sniper rifle with the M-82 telescopic sight in the hands of a properly trained sniper." A half dozen years later, Land commanded a sniper unit in Vietnam. It

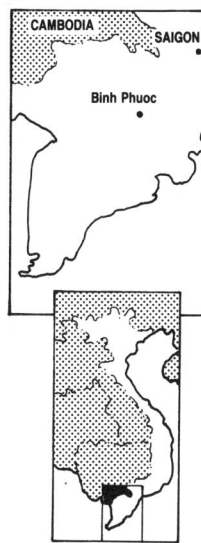

CAMBODIA   SAIGON

Binh Phuoc

Reach out and touch someone

AREA SCAN:
A Marine lance corporal searches the area around his outpost through the telescope of his bolt-action Model 700 Remington sniper rifle. It was the basic Marine sniper weapon. Army snipers preferred to use a self-loading rifle.

contained among other personnel Sergeant Carlos Hathcock who, with 93 confirmed kills, was the Marine Corps premier Vietnam-era sniper. At the outset a variety of weapons were employed by the Marine snipers. Where the Marine Corps ultimately decided in favor of a modified Model 700 Remington bolt-action rifle (in military terminology the M-40 Sniper rifle) as its basic sniper weapon, the Army's long distance shooters preferred to use a self-loading rifle.

In April 1967, the US Army Vietnam (USARV) announced to stateside organizations that it planned to conduct an evaluation of sniper operations and equipment. Building upon a year of ad hoc sniper activities, the USARV staff requested specific rifles and telescopes for issue to all Vietnam-based divisions and separate brigades for testing. Units

participating in the trials were directed by USARV
to develop their own training programs,
organizational structures, and tactical concepts for
the deployment of snipers. ACTIV personnel were
given the task of running the evaluation. Four
weapon systems were examined:

1. The Accurized 7.62 × 51mm NATO M-14 rifle
   with M-84 telescope. (This was a semiautomatic-
   only version of this rifle with carefully selected
   components, and the 2.5-power telescope usually
   mounted on the M-1D sniper rifle).

2. The 7.62 × 51mm NATO National Match M-14
   rifle with Limited War Laboratory adjustable
   ranging telescope. (This Redfield ART telescope
   was James Leatherwood's modification of a
   commercial 3 to 9 power model that incorporated
   a camming mechanism connected to the range-

finder so as to automatically zero the scope as the shooter adjusts the range to the target).

3. The 5.56 × 45mm M-16 rifle with Realist telescope. (A standard M-16 rifle with a 3-power Realist commercial scope).

4. 7.62 × 63mm Model 70 Winchester bolt-action rifle. (This was a .30-06 caliber sporting rifle with a commercial 3-power Weaver telescope.)

Most of the necessary weapons and scopes arrived in Vietnam by April 1967, the remainder—M-14 rifles with ART scopes—arrived in June. Data collection took place during the period July-October 1967.

Three of the four systems were unacceptable. During 7,512 man-days of weapon/scope use, 124 targets were engaged with the result of 46 KIA and 9 WIA.

The highest KIA to man-days ratio occurred in units that were operating primarily in the central highlands, coastal plain, and southern portion of the northern highlands. The lowest man-days to KIA ratio occurred in units employed in the lowlands north of Saigon and south of the central highlands.

At the end of the data collection period, 84 snipers (each having more than 60 days in combat operations) completed questionnaires about the equipment tested. The M-16 rifle with the Realist scope was the least favored, because it was inaccurate at ranges beyond 300 meters, moisture collected in its telescope, and the scope's inverted reticle was unacceptable. The M-14 rifle with the M-84 telescope was not liked because the telescope became fogged by moisture. The Winchester Model

BASIC EQUIPMENT:
The 7.62mm NATO XM-21 sniper rifle, with adjustable ranging telescope (ART) and telescope carrying case. The rifle was a specially modified version of the M-14.

70 rifle was reported to be too fragile for a combat environment and was also disliked because it would provide too little firepower in a combat situation. The clear favorite in this trial was the M-14 rifle with the ART scope.

The ACTIV team concluded that most units in Vietnam could profit from having snipers attached to them. The sniper was best associated with the rifle platoon, but occasionally it would pay to have a sniper assigned to brigade or battalion level. The National Match M-14 with the ART scope, if improved slightly for moisture-proofness and ruggedness, would make a suitable combat sniper rifle. Such a weapon needed to permit precise fire out to 600 meters, beyond that environmental and terrain conditions made it difficult to see targets. Suitable sniper training for US units could be conducted in Vietnam, provided a range with targets at 600 meters was available.

As a result, ACTIV evaluators recommended that snipers be added to the existing unit strength of American combat units in Vietnam. This would be an addition of firepower rather than a subtraction due to reassignment of regular riflemen. ACTIV also suggested that the Accurized M-14 with an improved telescope of the ART-type be fielded as quickly as possible. Nine months later, in June 1968, the 9th Infantry Division created the first sniper school in Vietnam. It was run by Major Willis L. Powell and eight noncommissioned officers from the Army Marksmanship Training Unit at Fort Benning, Georgia. Thirty students at a time were trained on the school's ranges, which were eventually extended

SOUND SECURITY: To reduce the vulnerability of the sniper, the US Army experimented with a number of sound suppressors. Here an XM-21 sniper rifle is fitted with a Sionics noise suppressor. While this device did not eliminate all of the sound made by the rifle, it did make the location of the weapon more difficult to determine.

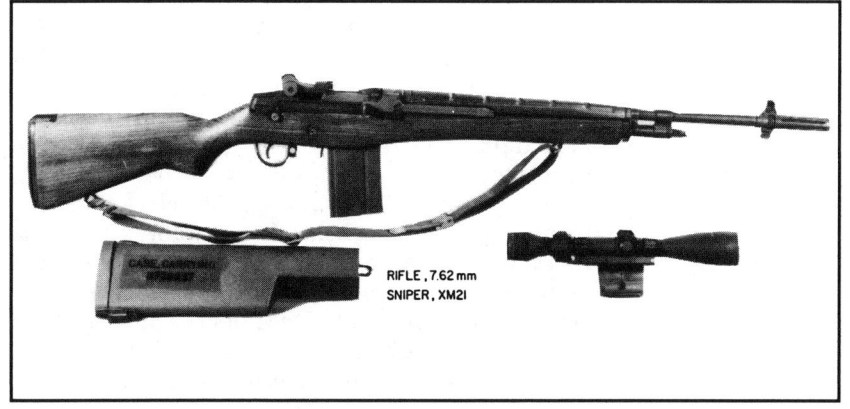

RIFLE , 7.62 mm
SNIPER , XM21

Reach out and touch someone

TEAMWORK:
A Marine sniper and his spotter working together scan the far bank of a river for VC activity. Snipers teams were especially successful in staging daytime ambushes, often establishing their own ambush sites from where they could hit targets up to 900 meters away.

to nearly 900 meters. Of the "expert" riflemen who volunteered for the rigorous course, only about half successfully completed it.

The first snipers graduated from the 9th Infantry Division's "Reliable Academy" in November 1968, and their first "kill" was recorded on 19 November at a location north of Binh Phouc in Long An Province. The second class of snipers were assigned to the field in early December, giving the Division a full complement of 72 snipers (six per battalion, and four per brigade). Despite all the close attention given to developing the 9th Infantry's sniper program, the early performance of the snipers themselves was uneven, with only eight kills in November and eleven in December. This was not a cost effective result for all the men and energy that had been dedicated to the program.

Senior commanders of the 9th Infantry Division set about analyzing equipment, personnel, methods, and tactics. The flaw was quickly apparent. At the outset snipers had been assigned by the battalions on the basis of two per line company. Company commanders had responsibility for the snipers but most company commanders did not know how to use them, nor did they care about their correct use. To remedy this problem, snipers were assigned to battalion headquarters, with the battalion commanders being responsible for proper utilization and emphasis on their sniper assets.

Once the individual battalion commanders began to assign their sniper teams to companies going on night operations, they began to obtain much better results. A sniper would report to a company commander, receive a briefing on the forthcoming

Reach out and touch someone

TEST SHOOT: An Infantry Board shooter takes aim with an XM-21 sniper rifle during military potential tests at Fort Benning, Georgia. This modified M-14 match rifle has an adjustable ranging telescope that simplifies the task of determining the distance to the target. Fort Benning's Army Marksmanship Training Unit provided the instructors for the first sniper school in Vietnam.

operation, and then he would select a promising area and wait for targets to appear. One of the most successful uses for these sniper weapons was daytime ambush patrols. Snipers would either accompany a platoon on an ambush, or they would establish their own ambush sites accompanied by a security element of five to eight riflemen. This technique paid off because snipers could and routinely did hit targets up to 900 meters away. Part of their effectiveness resulted from the fact that the Viet Cong were not used, at first, to US commanders deploying snipers.

Snipers also operated at night with the help of "pink light," illumination provided by infrared searchlights viewed through Starlight scopes.

Nighttime teams usually consisted of two snipers and two other soldiers armed with an M-16 rifle and

an M-79 grenade launcher. The team also carried
a radio. Snipers worked in pairs to reduce the eye
fatigue resulting from long periods of peering
through a Starlight night vision telescope.

Once the 9th Infantry Division's snipers began
to get personal attention and had the ability to hand
pick their shooting assignments, their day and night
results were extraordinary. In April 1969, the 80
snipers of the Division recorded 346 confirmed kills.
In subsequent months they averaged 200. In one
battalion (6th Battalion, 31st Infantry), during the
period 12 April to 9 May 1969, snipers killed 39 Viet
Cong (about 1.7 VC per engagement). The average
distance, because the operations were at night, was
148 meters and it required six shots per kill. Most
engagements occurred at 0400 hours. An unanticipated bonus from this was improved

A few of these self-loading Soviet 7.62 × 54mm Dragunov (SVD) sniper rifles were supplied to North Vietnamese snipers toward the end of the American phase of the Vietnam War. They were the first NVA sniper rifles to have a PSO-1 ranging and infrared detecting telescope.

performance on the part of US Army units operating at night. The effectiveness of their snipers gave the other men of the 9th Infantry Division additional confidence and aggressiveness.

Just as the Marine Corps had their top sniper, Sergeant Carlos Hathcock, the Army had a top shooter as well. Sergeant Adelbert F. Waldron, III, had 109 confirmed kills in just two months of shooting. Among his best shots was a kill made at 900 meters from a moving boat in the Mekong Delta. An enemy sniper made the mistake of firing at Sergeant Waldron. The Sergeant repaid him by shooting him out of his coconut tree nearly a kilometer away with a XM-21 sniper rifle. During his tour in Vietnam, Waldron was awarded two Distinguished Service Crosses for his skill and bravery.

Initially, the rifles used were National Match 7.62mm NATO caliber M-14 rifles. These rifles had glass bedded stocks for increased reliability and accuracy. Meanwhile, the ACTIV team's recommendations about the qualities desired in a combat sniper rifle led to a stateside decision in September

1968 to order 1,800 specially modified and Accurized M-14 National Match rifles fitted with Leatherwood's Adjustable Ranging Telescope (ART). This rifle preparation work involved both the US Army Limited War Laboratory and the US Army Materiel Command—the former organization prepared 65 rifles, while the latter modified 1,735 M-14s.

Getting snipers into combat became a priority. To speed up the process US commanders in Vietnam requested that 300 M-14 National Match Rifles be delivered immediately with the standard M-84 telescope. Subsequently, Rock Island Arsenal converted 1,435 M-14 National Match rifles, between October 1969 and March 1970, to the XM-21 configuration. Delivery of these sniper rifles was completed in March 1970, when 1,200 were shipped to Vietnam. This weapon was designated the XM-21 Sniper rifle, a designation it carried until December 1971 when it became the M-21 (Standard B). Reports back to the United States from troops in Vietnam were enthusiastic about the performance of the M-21 sniper rifle system.

Lieutenant General Julian J. Ewell, the 9th Infantry Division commander, noted that "the most effective single program we had was the sniper program. It took over a year from its inception in the States to its peak of performance in Vietnam. It also took plenty of hard work and belief in the concept and in our snipers. But more than anything it restored the faith of the infantryman in his rifle and in his own capabilities. Fighting alone at night without the usual available combined arms team, the 'rice paddy' soldier was more than a match for the enemy."

OLD STOCK:
For most of the war NVA snipers used this 7.62 x 54mm Soviet Model 1891/30 Mosin-Nagent bolt-action sniper rifle with its PU-Pe scope. Although it was a relatively old weapon, it proved to be a very accurate sniping rifle.

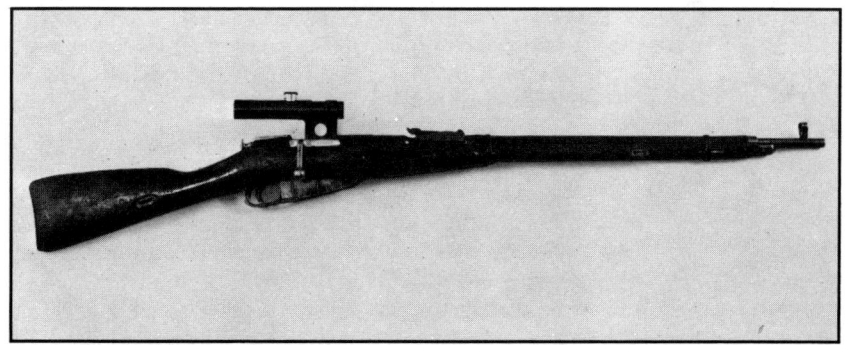

Riding the combat taxi

11

Mechanized Infantry

THE INTRODUCTION of American ground combat troops in 1965 led to the increasing use of infantry in a mechanized form. This led in turn to some battlefield hardware firepower innovations. For example, the absence of modern lightweight tanks resulted in the gradual evolution of the M-113 APC into a variety of light tank. These modifications began during the advisory period when the ACTIV personnel began to look for ways to improve the firepower of the M-113.

When it was originally introduced into combat, the M-113 had a single commander's hatch-mounted .50 (12.7mm) caliber M-2 Browning machine gun. Good for forward suppressive fire, this gun could not effectively be used to protect the APC from flank attack. Early on the ACTIV evaluators tested a three-position pedestal-mount base built by Rock Island Arsenal to take either the .30 caliber (7.62 × 63mm) M-1919A4 or the 7.62 × 51mm NATO M-60 machine guns. The virtue of this mount was the relative closeness at which the machine gunner could fire over the side of the M-113. In the M-60's most outboard position, the gunner could shoot at targets as close as 1.9 meters. Thousands of these mounts were subsequently fabricated by Rock Island Arsenal for use in Vietnam.

To fire a machine gun on this mount the gunner had to sit on the top of the M-113, exposed to enemy fire. To solve the problem six modified M-113s arrived in Vietnam for field tests on 29 April 1966. Each vehicle had four firing ports with observation

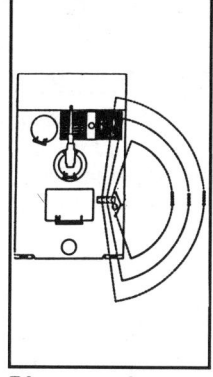

Diagram shows the field of fire provided by the three-position mount for .30 cal. and 7.62mm machine guns that allowed M-113 passengers to fire from the side of the vehicle for flank defense.

ACAV CONVERSIONS: APCs of Troop M, 3d Squadron, 11th Armored Cavalry Regiment take up defensive positions, using a flank-covering herringbone formation, after receiving sniper fire during Operation Cedar Falls in 1967. These M-113s are fitted with ACAV kits—a .50 cal. commander's gun and a 7.62mm M-60 general purpose machine gun.

ports on each side, two such ports on the rear ramp, a M-74C cupola (with twin .30 caliber (7.62 x 63mm) M-1919A4 machine guns); two side firing .30 caliber M-1919A4s, and special bar armor.

At the end of the two-month trial, all parties concerned agreed that the tropical Vietnamese climate made it unreasonable to expect troops to seal themselves inside an APC. "Because of the lack of an enemy air threat, the heat, and the threat of mines, it has become standard proceedure for ARVN personnel to ride on the top of the vehicle with hatches open rather than inside. If contact is made, all hatches remain open and any attached infantry dismount and fight on foot." ACTIV personnel concluded that side-mounted machine gun versions of the M-113, preferred by the ARVN, negated the need for firing/observation ports. The ACTIV evaluators recommended that "the M-113 armored personnel carrier not be modified by the addition of firing-observation port kits."

When the Americans of the reorganized 11th Cavalry (the 11th Armored Cavalry Regiment) entered the fray, in September 1966, they also experimented with beefing up the firepower of the

M-113. Slowly, that APC evolved into the ACAV (Armored Cavalry Assault Vehicle) through the addition of "armament subsystem kits." These Armored Cavalry Assault Vehicles came into being when American armored cavalry platoons were re-equipped with M-113s instead of tanks upon their arrival in Vietnam. Soon the men began modifying their APCs by building armored shields around the commander's .50 caliber M-2 machine gun and by adding pedestal mounts, complete with armored shields, for two side-mounted 7.62 × 51mm NATO caliber M-60 machine guns. There was also the addition of a removable pintel on the rear of the M-113 to serve as an alternative mounting for one of the M-60s. The "A" kit originated with the 11th Armored Cavalry, which had fitted its M-113s with them before arriving in Vietnam. A "B" kit, consisting of just the .50 caliber machine gun with shield, was used on the mortar carrier version of the M-113.

Field modified —An improvised shield provides protection for this M-113 commander and his .50 cal. (12.7 × 99mm) M-2 Browning heavy barrel flexible machine gun. Many vehicles were field modified before the ACAV kits became a standard issue set of equipment.

The use of the M-113 as an armed fighting vehicle was one of the major combat innovations during the Vietnam War. Originally, the M-113 APC had been intended to serve as a lightly armored combat taxi inside of which the infantry would ride to the frontline and then dismount to fight. In Vietnam, where there were no clearly identified front lines, American infantrymen, like the ARVN, rode into combat on the top deck of the M-113. From that position they could fire down upon the enemy when contact was made. Usually such contact came unexpectedly. Mounted like this they could benefit from the firepower of the ACAV's machine guns and the protection from mines, rockets, and booby traps provided by the body of the vehicle.

The APCs also helped troops physically push their way through the dense foliage without being directly exposed to the varied hazards—mines, punji sticks, and other booby traps—concealed in the undergrowth. While the .50 caliber and 7.62mm machine guns fired into the brush, the men atop the vehicles could further discourage the enemy by tossing hand grenades over the side. While far from perfect the ACAV gave the American and Vietnamese fighting men a slight advantage over the dismounted VC. New weapons, soon available to the VC, threatened to weaken that advantage.

Handheld and guided

CHAPTER

12

Antiarmor weapons

WITH THE APPEARANCE of US M-48 tanks, M-551 General Sheridan armored reconnaissance airborne assault vehicles, and additional M-113 APCs, the enemy leadership took steps to provide their troops with weapons that could effectively engage and destroy armored vehicles. Since their own number of armored vehicles was initially limited, and of little effect when put into battle, the NVA and Viet Cong looked for other ways of defeating US and ARVN armor. Although their antitank mines were reasonably effective, the NVA and VC discovered that they had the major tactical disadvantage of being passive weapons. The first effective antitank weapon which the Viet Cong introduced was the Chinese Type 36 57mm recoilless rifle.

This Type 36 was a close copy of the American M-18A1 developed in the closing stages of World War II. These Chinese 57mm recoilless weapons were well suited to guerrilla warfare, because they weighed only 20 kg and because they could be fired from the shoulder or from a machine gun tripod. The Type 36 fired a 1.23 kg shaped-charge antitank projectile, which could pierce through about 70mm of steel armor—twice the thickness of the aluminum plate of the M-113.

Although useless against modern main battle tanks, Type 36 recoilless rifles were fully capable of destroying the aluminum armor of the M-113. A hit on the body of an APC with a 57mm HEAT round generally put the vehicle out of operation and caused serious injuries to the crew and passengers. The Type 36's versatility as a weapon was further enhanced by its ability to fire antipersonnel high-explosive fragmentation shells and fire both

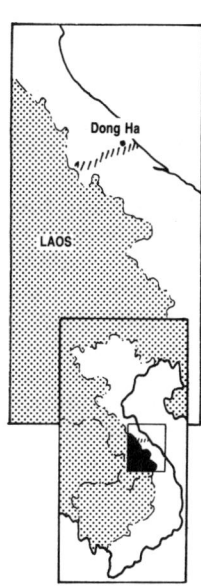

Chinese- and American-made ammunition, so that it could serve as both an antitank gun and an infantry support weapon.

Although less frequently encountered, the Chinese also provided the Type 52 75mm recoilless rifle, a copy of the US M-20, to their Vietnamese allies. This 52 kg weapon would also fire either American or People's Republic of China (PRC) ammunition. The slightly different Chinese Type 56 75mm recoilless rifle, a variant of the Type 52, fired only PRC ammunition. Neither of these weapons were the lightweight type of hardware suited to small units on foot.

The major defect of the Type 36, Type 52, and Type 56 recoilless rifles, as with all recoilless guns, was the back-blast that belched flame and smoke from the breech end when the weapon was fired. This "signature" immediately gave away the gunner's location. Counterfire was generally swift. Recoilless rifle gunners usually had to hold their fire until the target was very close. Consequently it was not unusual to lose either the gunner, the recoilless rifle, or both. The enemy soon realized that there was considerable value in acquiring a weapon that was more portable, more expendable, and less noticeable when used.

By the time of the Tet Offensive of 1968, new models of Soviet and Chinese recoilless weapons were being used by the NVA and some VC units. These included the Soviet B-10 (PRC Type 65) 82mm recoilless rifle, and the Soviet B-11 107mm recoilless

rifle. The former, with a gun weight of 57 kg, could project a 3.6kg warhead to nearly a kilometer, while the B-11, with a system weight of 305 kg, could deliver 9.0 and 13.6 kg projectiles over more than 6.5 kilometers. Their appearance in the NVA/VC arsenal coincided with the larger scale enemy operations of the final years of the conflict.

The use of recoilless guns was not confined to the NVA and Viet Cong. ARVN troops were equipped with a large number of US M-18A1 57mm recoilless rifles, some of which were mounted on M-113 armored personnel carriers. By war's end, more than 1,100 had been sent to South Vietnam by the United States. Late in the war both US and ARVN forces used the more modern and more powerful 90mm M-67 and 106mm M-40A1 recoilless rifles. These were used principally as direct-fire support weapons for infantry, especially when attacking enemy strongpoints. In the hands of the infantry company or battalion commander, these weapons provided an "instant artillery" capability. The M-67 was lighter, 16 kg vs 20.2 kg, and more effective than the 57mm M-18A1, with a maximum range of 2.1 kilometers. The M-40 series recoilless rifles could deliver a 7.7 kg payload to 7.7 kilometers.

The Viet Cong lost their first RPG-2 launchers to US and ARVN forces at the end of 1964. The first launchers recovered were PRC Type 56 launchers dated 1963. The North Vietnamese later made their own version of this weapon, calling it the B-40. The RPG-2 Ruchnoi protnivotankovi granatometi,

IMPROVED VERSION: An NVA soldier aims an RPG-7, the recoilless rifle that replaced the RPG-2. In addition to having a more sophisticated optical sight system, the RPG-7 had a stronger tube to accommodate the initiating recoilless launch charge of the PG-7 munitions.

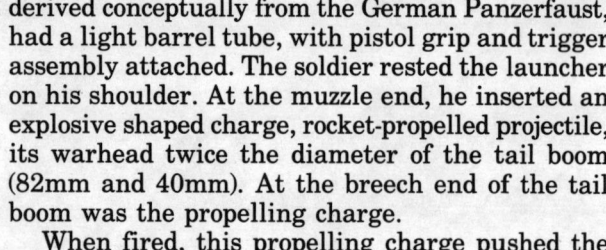

derived conceptually from the German Panzerfaust, had a light barrel tube, with pistol grip and trigger assembly attached. The soldier rested the launcher on his shoulder. At the muzzle end, he inserted an explosive shaped charge, rocket-propelled projectile, its warhead twice the diameter of the tail boom (82mm and 40mm). At the breech end of the tail boom was the propelling charge.

When fired, this propelling charge pushed the payload out the front. While there was the usual recoilless back-blast from the rear, it was less severe than that encountered with the Type 36 recoilless rifle. As the RPG-2's 1.84 kg missile moved toward the target a set of fins opened to stabilize its flight. The RPG-2 had an effective range of about 150-175 meters. On impact it could blast through armor at least three times as thick as that penetrated by the 57mm recoilless rifle shell, a capability that made it a serious threat to trucks, jeeps, and the M-113 APC.

In time, the Soviets replaced the RPG-2 with the RPG-7 (circa 1962), and it was used both as an anti-armor weapon and as a bunker buster. Although the RPG-7 resembled the RPG-2, it was a much more sophisticated and effective weapon. Its 85mm, 2.25 kg warhead could reach 920 meters before it self-destructed. Its shaped charge could defeat up to 330mm of armor plate. Today, 25 years later, it is still among the leading weapons of its class.

The principal difference between the RPG-2 and RPG-7 lay in the manner in which the projectile was driven forward. In the RPG-7, the projectile's launch was augmented by a recoilless charge that assisted the rocket motor. When the RPG-7 was fired, the recoilless charge hurled the rocket forward at low velocity. After about 15 meters of flight, the rocket motor ignited, accelerated, and sustained the projectile's flight. One of the reasons the Soviets created this two-step propulsion system was to protect the user and his fellow fighters from the back-blast of the rocket motor. A major drawback to this system was the extremely deafening report of the recoilless charge. Both the RPG-2 (Type 56) and the RPG-7 (Type 69) launchers were manufactured in North Vietnam (B-40 and B-41 respectively). All versions were used by NVA and VC forces in the last years of the war.

Rolling stock —Until the arrival of Soviet-built tanks in 1972, the Soviet B-10 82mm recoilless rifle was one of the few "mechanized" pieces in the NVA armory. The B-10 was a significant improvement in firepower over the Chinese Type 36 57mm and Type 52 75mm recoilless rifles. Although heavy (56.75 kg), its wheeled carriage made it possible to manhandle it through the most difficult terrain.

On the US and ARVN side of the conflict, the disposable 66mm M-72 HEAT rocket launcher, commonly called the "LAW," for light antitank weapon, provided a light compact weapon for use against armored and unarmored vehicles, fortifications, exposed troops, and other targets. Development of the M-72 LAW had begun in the mid-1950s, and the first version was standardized in March 1961, as a replacement for the older and more cumbersome M-20 series 3.5-inch (88mm) Bazooka. Unlike earlier reusable launchers, the one-shot M-72 was issued loaded in a collapsed configuration (656mm long), which was extended for firing (859mm). As issued it weighed 2.2 kg, and had a maximum range of 1,000 meters, with an 0.5 hit probability on a stationary target at 200 meters. Against exposed troops its warhead had a lethality roughly equivalent to the M-26 hand grenade.

Early M-72 Light Antitank Weapon launchers were extremely unsafe. If the weapon was armed, that is, if the launcher tube was extended for firing, there was the potential for an accidental discharge of the rocket when attempting to disarm it on returning it to the collapsed state. Stateside

ALLIED VERSIONS: Top: A South Korean soldier hauls a 57mm M-18A1 recoilless rifle across a river. The M-18A1 was used as a direct-fire support weapon providing instant frontline artillery. Below: An Air Cav trooper prepares to fire a 90mm M-67 recoilless rifle. It was lighter and more effective than the M-18A1, and had a maximum range of 2.1 kilometers.

experience, and Vietnam based evaluations in early 1968, led to a request for an improved M-72 LAW, known as the XM-72A1E1. Training with and evaluation of these LAWs took place between mid-March and the end of July 1969. XM-72A1E1 LAWs were fired in both simulated and combat situations. The improved LAW performed very well against buildings, bunkers, and exposed personnel. Despite complaints about the noise of the rocket at launch, the reports from troops who tested the improved LAW were positive about this rugged, reliable, and effective weapon. As a result, the XM-72A1E1, redesignated the M-72A2, became widely used by US and allied forces throughout Vietnam. More than 63,000 of these weapons fell into North Vietnamese hands at the end of the war.

In 1972, the North Vietnamese Army, as part of the buildup for a final offensive against the ARVN forces, added a third and far more dangerous weapon to its armory. In April of that year, the ARVN 20th Tank Regiment, operating near Dong Ha, near the DMZ in Quang Tri Province, with M-48 tanks, was attacked by NVA troops using the Soviet 9M-14M PTUR-64 Malatyuka (in NATO terminology ATGM-3 or "Sagger") guided missile. The Sagger was a semiautomatic command line-of-sight (SACLOS) guided weapon. In essence it was a wire-guided rocket carrying a very powerful shaped-charge warhead that was fired from a small launch pad placed on the ground away from the "gunner." The launch stand of the Sagger was connected by wire to a periscopic sight control unit. When the operator located a target and fired the rocket it

THE LAW:
An American serviceman takes aim with a 66mm M-72 Light AntiTank Weapon (LAW) that could destroy an enemy bunker in one blast. The size of its punch relative to its light weight made the LAW a popular weapon.

unreeled a fine wire connected to the control unit. The operator, looking through his sight, guided the weapon by pushing and twisting a control stick. The Sagger had a maximum range of 3,000 meters—the length of the wire—and could blast its way through 400mm of armor. In the first use of the Sagger, NVA soldiers destroyed an M-48 tank and an M-113 ACAV. But once the ARVN troops got over their initial surprise, they were able to locate the launch points and destroy the operators and control units.

The Sagger antitank missile system required a well-trained and cool individual for effective operation. Once the missile had been launched, the "gunner" had to "capture" the flying missile in his periscopic sight and then guide it to the target. Depending upon the skill of the gunner, and his distance from the launcher—up to 15 meters away—the missile could be captured at ranges of 500-800 meters from the point of launch. Under combat conditions, most gunners could only capture the missile and then engage targets beyond 1,000 meters. Nonetheless, the Sagger missile was lethal for tanks, and since it left the launcher armed, it could kill at very short ranges if it hit a target.

The introduction of the Sagger coincided with the reduction in US materiel support for South Vietnamese Armed Forces. As North Vietnam continued to build up its forces and improve its firepower, South Vietnam began to face serious ammunition shortages. The logistic tide turned in favor of the NVA and the VC, and the steady slide to a South Vietnamese defeat began.

WIRED DEVICE: Towards the end of the war, the North Vietnamese introduced the Soviet "Sagger" ATGM-3 antitank missile against American armored vehicles operated by ARVN troops. When it was fired the rocket unreeled a fine wire that kept it connected to the control unit from where it could be guided by a joystick towards the target.

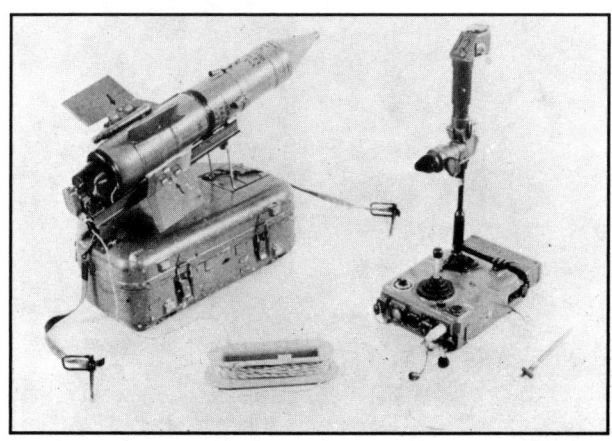

Winner takes all

13

Epilogue: North Vietnam's captured war surplus

HUGE QUANTITIES of weapons and related ammunition delivered to the armed forces supported by the United States were not enough to win the war in Southeast Asia. Nor were the tactical and materiel innovations developed in direct response to the enemy's methods of operation by the US Army for its men and those of the ARVN. The NVA and VC ultimately succeeded because their operating plan allowed them to retain the initiative through offensive actions. Northern forces tried until the post-1973 Paris Peace Agreement period to avoid US/ARVN strong points, choosing only to attack weak points. Sometimes they made deliberate attacks against strong allied positions when they had the requisite numerical advantage. Generally, they favored three basic tactical approaches—the raid, the ambush, and the attack by fire. Such encounters had the goal of inflicting casualties, and destroying equipment and installations, while wearing down the US/ARVN enthusiasm for the fight.

After US combat forces were introduced in South Vietnam in 1965, the NVA and the VC realized that it was beyond their capability to hold, occupy, or deny strategic positions. The only areas held with any degree of certainty were the cross-border sanctuaries in Cambodia, Laos, and North Vietnam. Knowing that the opposition possessed more firepower and mobility, Hanoi directed tactical commanders to mass, attack, and withdraw before allied forces could react. Some of these exercises were disasters. For example, the Tet Offensive of January-February 1968 was an expensive military disaster for the NVA and VC. While the North Vietnamese and the Viet Cong lost 37,000 troops

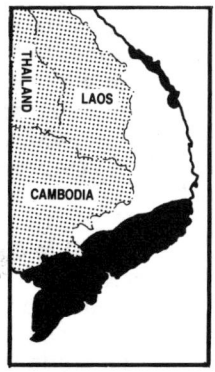

The final days —Areas marked in black were the last to fall, to the NVA, finally surrendering by April 30, 1975.

Winner takes all

CAPTURED STOCK:
Vast supplies of US weapons were sent to Vietnam from 1950 to 1975, making it inevitable that many would fall into enemy hands. Here VC guerrillas at Phu My Hung, a district less than an hour from Saigon, fight with a mix of weapons. One man is using a captured American 7.62 × 51mm NATO M-60 general purpose machine gun. His just visible comrade is armed with a 7.62 × 39mm AK-47.

killed and 6,000 more men wounded and captured, the ARVN lost only 2,082 and the Americans lost 1,001. But the domestic political tide in the United States was beginning to turn against the Americans. The American news media handled its reporting of the Tet Offensive in such a manner that it turned the NVA/VC battlefield defeat into a political victory.

The 30 years of conflict in Vietnam from 1945 to 1975 were played out on many stages. From the beginning the North Vietnamese realized the intricate relationship between the political and the military maneuver. Once portions of the American public began to campaign against the war, the North Vietnamese task was simplified. Secret negotiations between the United States and North Vietnam, begun in August 1969, led to President Richard M.

Nixon's speech to his nation on 25 January 1972 in which he announced that the United States would withdraw the remainder of its troops from South Vietnam. In the final agreement, the US had only 60 days to accomplish this task.

Ironically, removal of American troops followed a disastrous series of battlefield defeats for the NVA and VC in 1972. During that year, the North Vietnamese lost something in the order of 190,000 men. Of these 132,000 were killed in action, another 46,000 either died of wounds or were permanently disabled, 2,500 were taken prisoner, and 10,000 crossed over to the South Vietnamese side. Just as with the 1968 Tet counter-offensive, the allied victories of 1972 failed to alter American public opposition to the war. The political decision to extricate the United States from the Vietnam

WAR SURPLUS:
Since the fall of South Vietnam in 1975, those American small arms left behind have been pressed into service by the forces of the Socialist Republic of Vietnam. These members of a village self-defense force are carrying captured US 5.56 × 45mm M-16A1 rifles.

conflict remained unaltered. As the United States negotiated to remove its troops, the North Vietnamese sent over 148,000 fully equipped and supported replacements into the South. These regulars took over the fight for the Viet Cong who had been virtually eliminated in the 1972 US/ARVN campaigns.

As the Americans actually withdrew, the North Vietnamese continued to enhance their forces. By January 1973, there were between 160,000 and 170,000 North Vietnamese regular combat forces below the DMZ. They were backed by as many as 85,000 administrative and support personnel, and 41,000 members of the VC guerrilla infrastructure. In addition, the NVA had 70,000 regulars in Laos and 30,000 in Cambodia. The North Vietnamese withdrawal never materialized.

Instead, NVA logistic units began to upgrade the highway network leading south so still more and newer hardware could be moved into position. Modern heavy equipment was introduced in the South for the first time. Included were new APCs

(BTR-152), artillery tractors (M-2), new artillery (152mm D-20 gun-howitzer), and shoulder-fired surface-to-air antiaircraft missiles (SA-7). Remaining VC units were fully equipped with such weapons as AK-47s and RPG-2 and RPG-7 rocket launchers.

As American logistic support in the form of munitions and spare parts began to dry up, and the US Congress debated the proper levels of continued assistance, the NVA, unfettered by American air attacks on North Vietnam, Laos, or South Vietnamese segments of their supply network, were able to increase the tonnage of ammunition, tanks, and other heavy equipment along what had by now become the Ho Chi Minh "highway." It was precisely this unchallenged logistic system that provided the North Vietnamese with the military option of renewing the main force war when their political offensive failed.

United States materiel support for the ARVN had peaked in 1968-69 after the Tet Offensive. There was another surge of hardware in 1972 during the NVA offensive and allied counter-offensive of that year. At the time of the American withdrawal, there were more than adequate supplies of infantry small arms and support weapons. But ammunition was a problem. Following the 1973 "cease-fire," the fighting between ARVN and NVA was ferocious. South Vietnamese forces had lost 40,000 troops killed in action in 1972, from January to June 1973

TRAVELING GUN: According to official US records this 5.56mm M-16A1 rifle, serial number 1039301, was shipped to Cam Ranh Bay, South Vietnam, on 2 May 1968. In 1983 it was captured from anti-government forces by the Honduran Armed Forces during counter-insurgency operations. The exact path these Vietnamese-era weapons traveled is unknown, but it is thought that they arrived in Honduras via Nicaragua and probably Cuba.

they lost another 15,000 KIA, 5,000 dead from other causes, about 74,000 WIA, and 16,000 injured from noncombat causes. Many units were beginning to run low on such basics as 5.56mm rifle ammunition, 7.62mm machine gun ammunition, 40mm grenades, and 60mm and 81mm mortar rounds.

By mid-1974, concern about ammunition shortfalls turned to alarm. In February, the ARVN leadership concluded that at pre-cease-fire consumption rates they had only a 24-day supply of munitions. On average, between July 1974 and February 1975, in all categories, the ARVN had only a small fraction of the munitions available that they needed to sustain operations against the NVA. For the M-16 rifle they had 1.56 cartridges available per rifle per day. In 1972 they had expended on average 3.6 rounds per rifle per day. For 40mm grenades they had 0.2 per day vs. 0.8 expended in 1972. And for the M-72 LAW they had 4.5 per day vs. 84.4 per day actually expended in 1972 combat.

As the Viet Cong 514th Main Force Battalion had learned a decade before in the Mekong Delta, weapons without ammunition are worthless. Logistics were crucial to the outcome of the conflict. In the end the North Vietnamese won the logistic battle. And they won the war.

While all American forces brought their weapons back to the United States, when the Government of the Republic of South Vietnam collapsed in April 1975, substantial quantities of US military assistance materiel were lost to the Northern forces. Some of these weapons were removed from the

RECAPITULATION OF WEAPONS SUPPLIED TO ALLIED (NON-US) FORCES 1950-1975				
TYPE	VIETNAM	LAOS	CAMBODIA	TOTAL
Handguns	117,410	6,821	17,048	141,279
Submachine guns	1,374	11,718	3,092	16,184
Carbines and rifles	1,984,152	200,369	257,794	2,442,315
Shotguns	55,018			55,018
Machine guns	36,684	3,450	7,962	48,096
Grenade launchers	71,056	2,712	21,792	95,560
60mm Mortars	7,779	2,176	3,341	13,296

hands of ARVN troops (living and dead) by the NVA; some were already neatly stored in ARVN supply depots. Much of this materiel was new or in very good condition. Nearly all of it was operational.

During the past decade, the government of Vietnam has begun to release some of these arms into the international arena. By routes that are not clearly understood, some of these weapons have appeared in the hands of revolutionary and terrorist organizations in other countries, such as Chile, Colombia, El Salvador, Guatemala, and Honduras.

While there is no data available for 7.62mm M-73 armor machine guns or 12.7mm (.50) M-2 HB heavy machine guns (these weapons were generally associated with APCs and AFVs, and the quad .50 caliber machine gun M-55 trailer antiaircraft mount), substantial numbers are presumed to be still held by the Vietnamese. Also left behind were 63,000 M-72 66mm Light Antitank Weapons (LAW); 14,900 mortars (60mm and 81mm); 200 90mm M-67 recoilless rifles; 1,607 pieces of artillery (105mm, 155mm, and 175mm); 1,381 M-113 APCs; and 550 tanks (M-41A3 and M-48A3). In excess of 150,000 tons of ammunition were abandoned to the North Vietnamese.

If events of the past decade are any indication, these weapons will continue to be seen around the world for several decades. Thus the story of the small arms sent to Vietnam during the years 1945-75 is not completed. Just as with the war, the history of the infantry weapons has its many phases. The next phase will be recounted on some future battlefield.

US INFANTRY WEAPONS LEFT BEHIND IN VIETNAM AND CAMBODIA IN 1975

TYPE	VIETNAM	CAMBODIA	TOTAL
.45 cal. M-1911A1 pistols	90,000	24,000	114,000
5.56mm M-16A1 rifle	791,000	155,000	946,000
Mixed other rifles	857,580	104,000	961,580
7.62mm M-60 GM	15,000	320	15,320
40mm M-79 grenade launcher	47,000	18,500	65,500

AAA	— Antiaircraft artillery.
ACAV	— Armored Cavalry Assault Vehicle.
ACTIV	— Army Concept Team In Vietnam.
AK-47	— Soviet 7.62mm automatic assault rifle (Kalashnikov).
AO	— Area of operations.
APC	— Armored Personnel Carrier.
ARPA	— Department of Defense's Advanced Research Projects Agency.
ART	— Adjustable Ranging Telescope.
ARVN	— Army of the Republic of Vietnam.
ATGM	— Antitank Guided Missile.
BAR	— Browning Automatic Rifle.
Battery	— Artillery unit equivalent to infantry company.
Bde	— Brigade.
Bn	— Battalion.
BRL	— Ballistic Research Laboratories.
Bunker	— Fighting position with overhead cover.
CCT	— Command and control team.
Charlie	— Nickname for the Viet Cong.
Chicom	— Chinese Communist.
CIDG	— Civilian irregular defense group.
Claymore	— Command-detonated antipersonnel mine.
Co	— Company.
CO	— Commanding officer.
COSVN	— The Vietnamese Communist headquarters.
CROW	— Counter Recoil Operated Weapon.
CSWS	— Crew Served Weapon Night Sight.
DMZ	— Demilitarized Zone.
DRV	— Democratic Republic of Vietnam (North Vietnam).
ENSURE	— Expediting Non-Standard Urgent Requirements for Equipment.
GLAD	— Grenade Launcher Attachment Development.
HE	— High explosive.
IR	— Infrared.

IRB	— Infrared binoculars.
KIA	— Killed in action.
LAW	— Light Antitank Weapon.
LMG	— Light machine gun.
LRRP	— Long-range reconnaissance patrol.
LZ	— Landing zone.
M-16	— Automatic 5.56mm rifle.
M-48	— Medium tank.
M-60	— 7.62mm machine gun.
M-79	— Grenade launcher.
M-113	— Armored personnel carrier.
MAAG	— Military Assistance Advisory Group.
MACV	— Military Assistance Command, Vietnam.
MAS	— Manufacture d'Armes de Saint-Etienne.
MAT	— Manufacture d'Armes de Tulle.
MG	— Machine gun.
NOD	— Night Observation Device.
NVA	— North Vietnamese Army.
PRC	— People's Republic of China.
PF	— Popular Forces.
RF	— Regional forces.
RPG	— Rocket-propelled grenade.
RTO	— Radio-telephone operator.
Sapper	— NVA or VC trained in demolitions.
SMG	— Submachine gun.
Tet	— Vietnamese lunar New Year.
USARV	— US Army Vietnam.
USMC	— US Marine Corps.
Vietminh	— Contraction of Viet Nam Doc Lap Dong Minh Hoi, or League for the Independence of Viet Nam. Established in 1945 and dominated by communist forces led by Ho Chi Minh, it fought for independence against the French.
VC	— Viet Cong.
Vietnamization	— Handing the war over to the South Vietnamese.
WHA	— Wounded by hostile action.

About the Author

Edward C. Ezell

EDWARD C. EZELL is a historian of military technology specializing in the development and use of military small arms. Currently he is Supervisory Curator of the Armed Forces History Division at the National Museum of American History, Smithsonian Institution, Washington, DC. Dr. Ezell is the author of several histories of military small arms. These include *Handguns of the World: Military Revolvers and Self-Loading Pistols* (1981), *The Great Rifle Controversy: Search for the Ultimate Infantry Rifle from World War II to Vietnam and Beyond* (1984; revision of 1969 doctoral dissertation), and *The AK-47 Story: Evolution of the Kalashnikov Weapons* (1986).

He has also edited the 11th and 12th editions of *Small Arms of the World: A Basic Manual of Small Arms* (1977 and 1983) and the 1st and 2nd editions of *Small Arms Today: Latest Reports on the World's Small Arms* (1984 and 1988).

In addition to six years of college teaching, and six years as a historian with the National Aeronautics and Space Administration, he was Vice President in charge of Interarms Asia's operations out of Singapore during the latter years of the Vietnam War (1972-74). Since 1986, he has been a director of the Institute for Research on Small Arms in International Security located in Washington, DC.

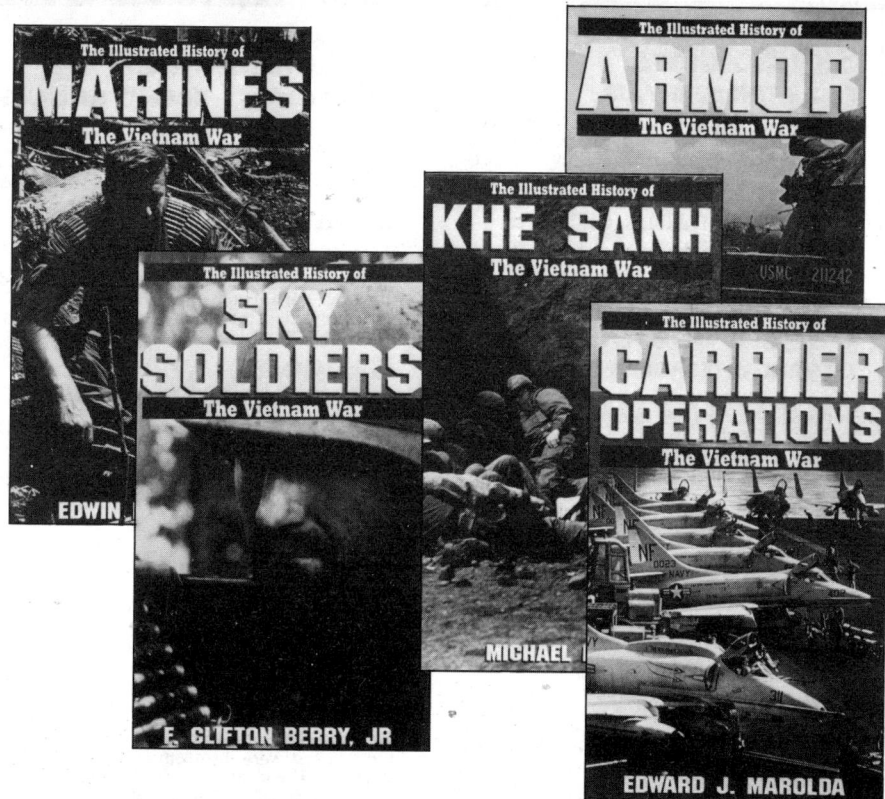

The Illustrated History of
MARINES
The Vietnam War

EDWIN

The Illustrated History of
ARMOR
The Vietnam War

USMC 211242

The Illustrated History of
KHE SANH
The Vietnam War

The Illustrated History of
SKY SOLDIERS
The Vietnam War

F. CLIFTON BERRY, JR

The Illustrated History of
CARRIER OPERATIONS
The Vietnam War

MICHAEL

EDWARD J. MAROLDA

THE ILLUSTRATED HISTORY OF THE VIETNAM WAR

Bantam's Illustrated History of the Vietnam War is a unique and new series of books exploring in depth the war that seared America to the core: a war that cost 58,186 American lives, that saw great heroism and resourcefulness mixed with terrible destruction and tragedy.

The Illustrated History of the Vietnam War examines exactly what happened. Every significant aspect—the physical details, the operations, and the strategies behind them—is analyzed in short, crisply written original books by established historians and journalists.

Some books are devoted to key battles and campaigns, others unfold the stories of elite groups and fighting units, while others focus on the role of specific weapons and tactics.

Each volume is totally original and is richly illustrated with photographs, line drawings, and maps.